D1032456

No Way Out

No Way Out

Persistent Government Interventions in the Great Contraction

Edited by Vincent R. Reinhart

The AEI Press

Publisher for the American Enterprise Institute

WASHINGTON, D.C.

Distributed by arrangement with the Rowman & Littlefield Publishing Group, 4501 Forbes Boulevard, Suite 200, Lanham, Maryland 20706. To order, call toll free 1-800-462-6420 or 1-717-794-3800. For all other inquiries, please contact AEI Press, 1150 Seventeenth Street, N.W., Washington, D.C. 20036, or call 1-800-862-5801.

Library of Congress Cataloging-in-Publication Data

No way out : persistent government interventions in the great contraction / edited by Vincent R. Reinhart.
    pages cm
  Includes bibliographical references.
    ISBN 978-0-8447-4358-5 (cloth) — ISBN 978-0-8447-4359-2 (pbk.) — ISBN 978-0-8447-4360-8 (ebook) 1. Global Financial Crisis, 2008–2009— Government policy. 2. Global Financial Crisis, 2008–2009—Government policy—United States. 3. Bank failures—Law and legislation—United States. 4. Financial crises—Prevention. 5. Economic stabilization—International cooperation. I. Reinhart, Vincent, editor of compilation.
    HB37172008 .N6 2013
    339.509'0511—dc23
                                                            2012051370

Printed in the United States of America

Contents

List of Illustrations

Figures

Tables

Preface

Vincent R. Reinhart

In 2009, one-half of the world's economies were in recession. Indeed, 95 percent of world output was in places where contractions were occurring. That year, and the immediate aftermath of sluggish recovery and tepid expansion, shows that a severe financial crisis leaves a long wake on the economic waters. But the cost of a crisis does not end after output finally and grudgingly recovers its previous peak. In fact, there are two long-lasting tolls.

First, financial crises recur regularly enough throughout history that Carmen Reinhart and Kenneth Rogoff (2009) thought the irony would be obvious in the title of their eight-hundred-year history, *This Time Is Different*. Despite the repetition of crises, policymakers improvise time and time again. In financial rescues, serious people in power seem to view ambiguity as constructive. Learning by doing, however, can prove expensive when billions of dollars are on the line and little thought is given to precedent. In 2008 and 2009, government protections were given to institutions solely because they were deemed too big to fail, after-the-fact insurance was provided to money-market mutual funds that had paid no insurance premiums, and trillions of dollars of liquidity were lent to private foreign financial institutions without prior consultation with Congress. Profit seekers in the private sector will no doubt learn what to expect from the government in the future. Their decisions will be different as they adjust to the new regulatory environment and try new profit-making strategies, and future government officials will be placed in similarly difficult positions.

Second, the heat of a crisis often prompts action without thought of the longer-term effort required to reverse those actions. From 2008 to 2010, the federal government added almost $5 trillion to its stock of debt, partly as the result of massive fiscal stimulus. The Federal Reserve more than trebled its balance sheet in an attempt to provide monetary stimulus through quantitative easing. And the US government took ownership stakes in many important financial and industrial firms. How we disentangle ourselves from those commitments will determine the amount of resources available for other problems of public policy. This, in turn, will shape the public's attitudes toward the size of the government, the role of free enterprise, and the relative importance of opportunity and security.

At the time of the crisis, neither thinking about the precedent nor planning the exit seems to be the appropriate way to conduct public policy. Even more worrisome, as time passes, we forget, which is one reason financial crises return with discouraging regularity. Indeed, the crisis of 2008 is not much a topic of current public discourse.

To fill the void and press for a more encompassing understanding of the precedent of crisis management and the need to plan an exit, the American Enterprise Institute commissioned papers on a variety of these topics. We began by developing competing narratives. These narratives must be refined to form the body of knowledge that will help us prevent and prepare for future crises.

This book represents an effort to gather these competing narratives and provide a varied, but cohesive, story of the crisis. The essays contained within vary in style, from full-fledged research papers to commentaries, and cover a range of topics, from the global impact of the banking crisis to its impact on fiscal and monetary policy. However, they all provide a different perspective on the causes, outcome, and policy implications of the crisis.

My introductory essay provides a good starting place. I discuss the financial crisis from its beginning to 2009, starting with the factors that led to the housing bubble and how it propagated into the general economy. I then examine how this domestic downturn spread to a global scale and the policy options, fiscal and monetary, that US officials undertook while attempting to address the growing unemployment rate.

Christopher Whalen follows with a fiery piece on the power of free markets and the need for a political system that will allow free markets to bloom. He criticizes Congress and the president for bailing out banks and promoting a culture of too big to fail. He provides an alternative view for the future, where free markets and destructive capitalism promote growth and strength in the United States.

Next, Angel Ubide looks at how the financial crisis of 2008 undermined many of the key paradigms of financial economic thought, leaving economic scholars baffled as the banking sector collapsed. As he explains, "All of a sudden, we did not know anymore how the world operated." While this baffled policymakers and paralyzed markets at the time, the dust has begun to settle, revealing several preliminary lessons for policymakers.

Greg Ip looks at the sources and causes of this crisis from a global perspective. Dismissing the traditional culprits, Ip examines why certain countries were hit harder than others. He finds that the United States' large "shadow banking" sector and dedication to promoting homeownership led to the housing bubble, while global interconnections allowed the crisis to spread from country to country.

Frederic S. Mishkin examines the changing role of the Federal Reserve in the aftermath of the crisis. The Fed took on a much larger role in regulating banks and influencing the financial sector in response to the unfolding events of this recession, and Mishkin looks at why the Fed would make a good or bad regulator, and the implications it would have on the Fed's independence. Finally, he responds to criticisms of macroeconomic research as a field of study and calls for the beginning of "a new golden era of macroeconomics."

Ethan Ilzetzki, Enrique G. Mendoza, and Carlos A. Végh change pace by addressing fiscal policy and the discordant views on the magnitude of fiscal policy multipliers. Using cross-country regressions, they find that many different factors affect multipliers, including the exchange-rate regime, debt load, and a country's openness to international trade, as well as intertemporal differences.

Ricardo Reis, like Mishkin, looks at the changes that have occurred at the Federal Reserve in response to the financial crisis and ensuing recession, in particular the expansion and diversification of its balance sheet. Looking to the past, Reis considers the growing role of the Fed in the financial markets and discusses the dangers of this expansion—both to the economy, through the possibility of higher inflation or unemployment, and to the

Fed, through a potential loss of independence. Looking to the future, he speculates on the future of the Fed, whether it can or should return to its previous role, and the difficulties and dangers of attempting to scale back the Fed's role in the economy.

Michael D. Bordo and John Landon-Lane present an in-depth look at recessions in the United States in order to study the proper policy responses in the aftermath of a crisis. Using both descriptive and empirical evidence, they examine previous policy responses to an improving economy to see how soon the Fed begins tightening its policy after the improvement of several macroeconomic indicators. Their findings provide insight into what the proper policy response will be as our economy begins its slow progress toward normalcy.

Finally, a forward-looking essay by Francis E. Warnock discusses the financial crisis that did not happen—a worldwide withdrawal from US investments that would cause global imbalances in finance and trade. These concerns were shared by many economists before the current recession, which caused confusion when US securities flourished during the recent crisis. Warnock looks at why foreign investors continued to support American investments, and whether this problem will be of further concern in the future.

1

Introduction: The Origin, Propagation, and Magnification of the Financial Crisis: A Prospectus for the *No Way Out* Project

Vincent R. Reinhart

President John F. Kennedy famously said that "victory has one-thousand fathers, but defeat is an orphan."[1] The financial crisis of 2007–2009 suggests a corollary to his advice. Defeat may be an orphan, but it has more than a thousand biographers. Scores of financial writers, academics, and other analysts are in the process of interpreting recent strains in financial markets and policy actions by high officials and positing a range of different implications for the global economy.

Those competing narratives are not just about book sales. Society is in the process of drafting a narrative to explain what just happened. The story that is settled on will determine the legislative and regulatory response in the near term, as well as attitudes toward financial instruments and intermediaries over the longer term.

Thus far, the evolving narrative has been narrow and focused inward on the United States. At one level, this seems natural because the story usually starts with excesses in residential construction and mortgage finance here at home. However, a purely domestic discussion falls short on two counts. First, while the fickle nature of financial markets seems unprecedented after almost three decades of "great moderation" in advanced economies, it has remained commonplace in emerging-market economies. Thus, looking to that more varied experience can help us understand the macroeconomics of high volatility. Second, and probably more important, a domestic focus neglects the important role of the international sector in both fostering initial excesses and propagating the correction. Such channels of propagation are essential in understanding how the initiating downturn in the US housing market, while large relative to economic activity, produced a stunning contraction in global financial markets. Understanding the appropriate role of the international sector will also reveal policy opportunities to facilitate recovery, not all of which have been taken.

Five sections follow. First, **the origin of the problem** will be traced to excesses in the housing market, which were fueled by financial innovation, governmental encouragement, and ample global saving. Open financial markets did precisely what theory has predicted ever since Robert Mundell observed that market interest rates were increasingly related to world conditions, not those in any particular country. Thus, the scope for uncoordinated domestic action by the Federal Reserve was limited.

Second, **the domestic downturn** initially played out as a sharp correction in one sector that had allowed excesses to accumulate over a decade. A correction in a $27 billion asset class would naturally involve large numbers, but this crack in financial markets widened through the domestic economy.

Third, the propagation and magnification of the downturn owed importantly to global linkages. The United States was not alone in having a burning-hot real estate market, in part because it had exported some of its innovations in housing finance. More fundamentally, trade linkages have turned out to be very important. The left panel of figure 1-1 plots monthly world exports since 2007. The format is a radar chart, where monthly values are displayed along the rays. The spiraling inward of world trade over the past two years mirrors the experience from 1929 to 1933 in a chart made famous by the League of Nations Economics Unit.

The international propagation of the shock also owed to an essential aspect of the financial world: support for a particular market depends on participants' expectations about the behavior of others. In general, this sets the stage for multiple equilibria and herding. In this particular case, the thundering herd all attempted to leave the plain at once. With the possibility of a self-reinforcing withdrawal from markets, liquidity can be ephemeral. That is not a lesson unknown to reserve managers in many emerging-market economies that are prone to "sudden stops" of foreign capital, to use Guillermo Calvo's phrase.[2] It was, however, news to US officials.

FIGURE 1-1

WORLD EXPORTS

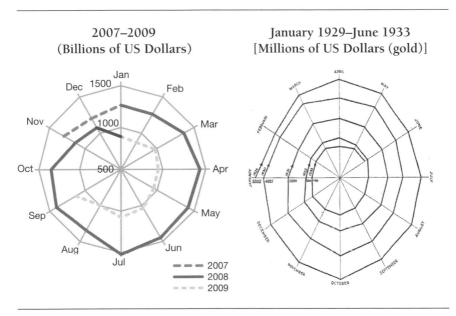

2007–2009
(Billions of US Dollars)

January 1929–June 1933
[Millions of US Dollars (gold)]

- - - 2007
——— 2008
- - - 2009

SOURCES: IMF International Financial Statistics and League of Nations Economic Survey.

Fourth, **policy actions** spanned significant use of fiscal, monetary, and financial policies as all hands were put on deck. The Obama administration and Congress acted in a timely fashion to provide fiscal stimulus, but the effectiveness was questionable given the composition and profile of the initiatives. Indisputable is the consequence for the public debt, which is thus far following an upward track. The Federal Reserve aggressively pulled its policy rate down and then resorted to an unconventional expansion of its balance sheet. Such aggressive use of macro policy tools, especially fiscal ones, has precedent, as does the unfortunate tendency to withdraw support prematurely.

The record is much less favorable on direct financial actions to deal with the crisis. Interventions were haphazard at first, as officials confused a fundamental solvency problem for one of illiquidity. Other mistakes included ambiguity about the perimeter of aid and inflammatory public statements. Policy was not coordinated across countries, although there were numerous examples of policy emulation as action in one country—in a world with open borders to international capital flows—forced action elsewhere.

Most problematic is that officials in many countries seemed satisfied to delay recognition of the losses on the balance sheets of their national financial champions. The precedent for such forbearance is forbidding.

Fifth, the **opportunities for additional policy action** on the global stage remain significant.

The Origins of the Downturn

Amid the wreckage in financial markets, it is easy to forget that the US housing market had a remarkable decade-long run. Single-family house permits, for instance, shown in figure 1-2, more than doubled over the fourteen-year period beginning in 1991.

Fundamentals supported housing demand for much of the 1990s and early 2000s. The growth of real disposable income was solid. Real mortgage

FIGURE 1-2

NEW PRIVATELY OWNED HOUSING UNITS STARTED

(THOUSANDS OF UNITS)

SOURCE: US Census Bureau.

interest rates were low. Demographics were favorable, in that the baby-boom generation was aging, which led them to trade up their housing stock and made them desirous of second homes. The country also had a large influx of immigrants a decade earlier, and those permanent residents were seeking starter homes. This created a strong demand for housing and opportunities for capital gains that reinforced that demand.

Financial encouragement of home purchases shifted real resources, toward this growing demand. Total employment in construction and finance, shown in figure 1-3, increased from 10.25 percent of the work-force in 1992 to 11.75 percent by 2006. This is a huge shift in resources considering that the denominator in this calculation is currently about 137 million workers. The steep decline following the crest can be attributed almost entirely to downturns in employment in the financial sector, which lost over 16 percent of its 2006 workforce. The housing boom also set up a potential tension, in that the resources used to build houses adjust only

FIGURE 1-3

EMPLOYMENT IN CONSTRUCTION AND FINANCE
(AS A SHARE OF ALL EMPLOYEES, PERCENTAGE)

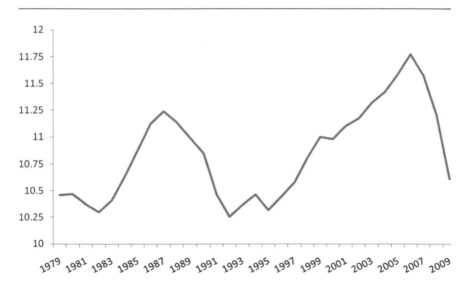

SOURCE: Bureau of Labor Statistics. Data for 2009 are preliminary.

sluggishly, while the price of their final product can adjust more rapidly in the manner of an asset price.[3]

The market for residential housing, of course, does not follow the paradigms of rationality all that closely, as noted by Case and Shiller (1989), and is regional in nature. And some regions were indeed hot, feeding speculation. As shown in figure 1-4, house prices appreciated significantly from 1995 to 2006 across all regions of the country, but especially notable were the three-figure rates in the Southeast and the West. The high reading from the nineteen regions of the Case-Shiller price index, available since 1995, was recorded in Los Angeles at 266 percent. The low, in Cleveland, still represented nearly a 5 percent annual rate of return. The allure of capital gains can be powerful, and in ways not always captured in the conventional rational-expectations paradigm.[4]

As has been the case for some time, the US government provides considerable encouragement to homeownership, beginning with the tax deductibility of mortgage interest payments. Both the volume and direction of mortgage flows were partly influenced by the financial equivalent of the Army Corps of Engineers in the US government that dredged channels of funding and built up levees of levered resources. The housing-related government-sponsored enterprises (GSEs) facilitated mortgage borrowing by creating a market for mortgage securitization and by holding large volumes of whole loans and securities on their own books. The Federal Reserve aided those entities by granting the GSEs direct access to the payment system and facilitating the clearing and settling of their securities. Regulatory guidance encouraged housing activity, especially in underserved areas. This encouragement was formalized in the Community Reinvestment Act, reporting requirements in the Home Mortgage Disclosure Act, and affordable-housing guidelines for the GSEs.

The two vintages of the Survey of Consumer Finances (SCF) taken in 2004 and 2007 show that upper-income households were the ones who most forcefully followed the government's advice to take levered bets on housing. As shown in figure 1-5, it was among households in the sixtieth to ninetieth percentiles of the income distribution where the share of those holding debt secured by a primary residence increased the most.

But those households were not alone. Opportunities for wealth creation in the United States are less plentiful at the lower end of the income

FIGURE 1-4

HOME PRICES IN MAJOR CITIES
(CHANGE OVER SELECTED PERIOD, PERCENTAGE)

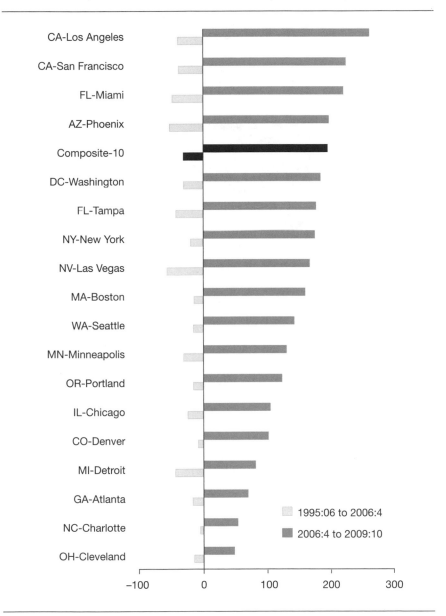

SOURCE: Case-Shiller/S&P.

FIGURE 1-5
DEBT SECURED BY PRIMARY RESIDENCE

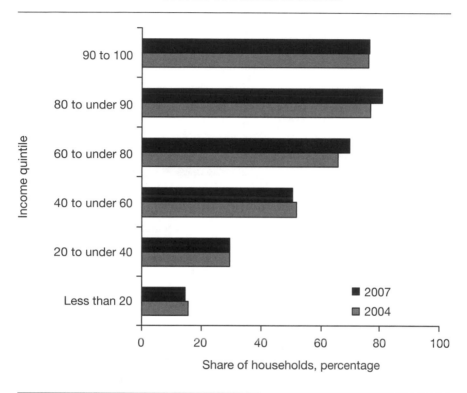

SOURCE: Federal Reserve, Survey of Consumer Finances.

distribution. For instance, looking at the SCF conducted in 2007, direct-equity holdings are concentrated in the top quintile of the income distribution (the first column in table 1-1). Lower down the income distribution, people do not hold equities. But people in all income brackets have homes. About 41 and 55 percent, respectively, of all households in the lowest and next-lowest income quintile own homes (the second column in table 1). As a consequence of this focus on property, households are underdiversified.[5] As the third column shows, except for households in the highest income bracket, homes constitute about one-half of assets. Constrained choice among those with lower incomes made even more appealing the invitation

TABLE 1-1
FAMILY HOLDINGS OF FINANCIAL ASSETS IN 2007 (PERCENTAGE)

| Across percentile of income | Share of families holding asset | | House values as a share of all assets |
	Direct stock	Primary residence	
Less than 20 percent	5.5	41.4	47.1
20 to under 40 percent	7.8	55.2	51.8
40 to under 60 percent	14	69.3	48.4
60 to under 80 percent	23.2	83.9	45.3
80 to under 90 percent	30.5	92.6	44.5
90 to 100 percent	47.5	94.3	19.8

SOURCE: Federal Reserve, Survey of Consumer Finances.

to use leverage (in the form of a home mortgage) to tap an asset class where there had been a rapid run-up in prices.

International capital flows facilitated the funding of this housing boom. Many observers noted that the US current account deficit seemed on an unsustainable track in the late 1990s and thereafter.[6] Indeed, as plotted by the line in figure 1-6, the current account balance bulked to less than minus 4 percent of nominal gross domestic product (GDP) by the end of the last decade and subsequently deteriorated. As other observers noted, however, the US current account deficit would only become unsustainable once foreigners became less willing to continue to add to their holdings of US obligations. Some doubted that this appetite would wane.[7] In fact, after the Asian crisis that began in 1998, official foreign entities increased their purchases of reserve assets (see the bars in figure 1-6).[8] Those official purchases tilted heavily toward US government securities. According to the Currency Composition of Official Foreign Exchange Reserves (COFER), a survey by the International Monetary Fund (IMF), about two-thirds of official reserve assets were held in US dollars, on average, over 1997–2008.[9]

Thus, foreigners seemed willing to accommodate increased US demands on their saving. One way of seeing this more starkly is to compare the net creation of US Treasury securities—that is, the negative of the federal

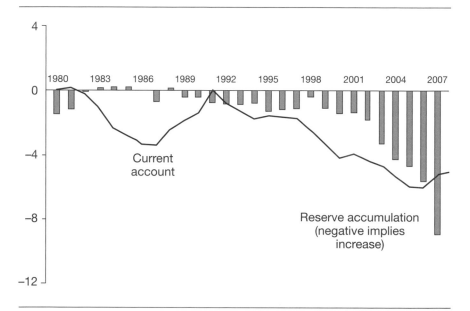

FIGURE 1-6

US CURRENT ACCOUNT BALANCE AND RESERVE
ACCUMULATION BY EMERGING-MARKET ECONOMIES
(RELATIVE TO US NOMINAL GDP, PERCENTAGE)

SOURCE: IMF, *World Economic Outlook* (October 2009).

deficit—to an estimate of net additions of dollar assets in foreign official reserves, as shown in figure 1-7. The solid line plots an estimate of foreign official purchases of US government securities, which is just the average of dollar reserves, from the COFER, making up two-thirds of the total multiplied by the total reserve acquisition. Note that, in many years, foreign official accounts appeared willing to fund the entire US federal deficit.

This willing funding by foreign official accounts altered the composition of finance and kept the level of long-term interest rates in the United States low. First, as for the compositional effect, foreign official entities loaded up on US government securities, leaving private demands unmet. Into this void, financial engineers constructed AAA-rated dollar exposure. How did they do that? They used housing collateral to create mortgage-backed securities and collateralized mortgage obligations. The top tiers of those

FIGURE 1-7

NET CREATION OF US TREASURY SECURITIES AND
NET ADDITIONS TO FOREIGN US DOLLAR RESERVES
(RELATIVE TO US NOMINAL GDP, PERCENT)

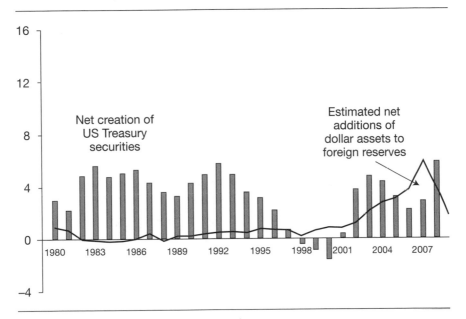

SOURCE: IMF, *World Economic Outlook* (October 2009).

payment flows were rated by the rating agencies as AAA, meeting the need, particularly, of foreign banks that were desirous of those securities' special treatment under the Basel II capital rules.

This posed a problem for the investment banks that put in motion the process of financial engineering. Underwriting these complicated securities to meet the demand of foreigners for AAA-rated credit left them with bits and pieces of securities on the cutting-room floor. This unwanted residue of their own underwritings represented highly leveraged bets on the US housing market that proved difficult to remove from their balance sheets. An attractive route was to park these items in special purpose vehicles—entities set up with purportedly enough capital and distance from the mother ship to be treated as completely off the corporate balance sheet, according to accounting rules. Accounting rules, however, were not reality. In their

FIGURE 1-8

FOREIGN EXPOSURE TO US PRIVATE CREDIT
(SHARE OF TOTAL US ASSETS HELD BY THE FOREIGN SECTOR, PERCENTAGE)

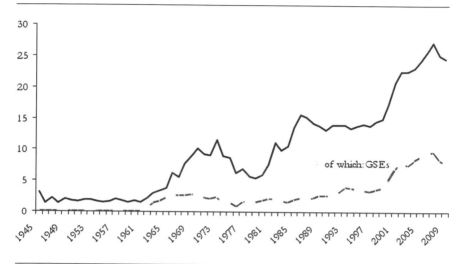

SOURCE: Federal Reserve, Flow of Funds Accounts.

death throes, the special purpose vehicles crawled back to their creator. Therein was one of the major and sudden sources of deterioration in the balance sheets of key institutions.

One way of seeing this increased interest of the foreign private sector in nongovernmental securities is provided in figure 1-8. The solid line plots foreign holdings of US private credit, as a share of total holdings of US assets abroad. Foreign exposure to the US credit market increased by about 15 percentage points in 1999–2009. As shown by the dashed line, the GSEs were important in those net additions. They marketed global securities to fund a housing boom in increasing volume, just as the boom was beginning to tail out.

The second main consequence of these global savings was to keep US long-term interest rates lower than they would have been otherwise. Indeed, as shown by the solid line in figure 1-9, the ten-year Treasury yield remained in a narrow range for at least a decade, even as the federal funds rate—the dashed line—dipped, rose, and then dipped again.

FIGURE 1-9

FEDERAL FUNDS AND TEN-YEAR TREASURY RATES

(PERCENTAGE)

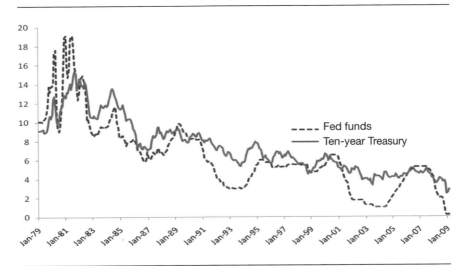

SOURCE: Federal Reserve Bank of St. Louis, Federal Reserve Economic Data (FRED). From December 16, 2009, to the present, the federal funds target is a range from zero to twenty-five.

The figure suggests that the longer-term market rate, which presumably matters for private spending decisions, seemed to become disconnected from the policy rate, the Fed's main lever on the economy. Table 1-2 shows the simple correlation between monthly changes in the federal funds and the ten-year Treasury rates in the first column and the thirty-year fixed-rate mortgage rate in the second column. Back in the 1980s, the first rows, changes in the federal funds rate were predictably associated with changes in longer-term yields, with a correlation on the order of one-half. In the era of the housing boom, however, from 1996 to 2006, the effective correlation was zero.

Any analyst pointing to Federal Reserve policy as augmenting the housing boom must first address how the Federal Reserve might have had the leverage to do so.[10] In the event, the simple correlation from 2002 to 2006 between its policy instrument and the rate that matters for housing activity was negative and statistically insignificant from zero. Perhaps this reduced-form coefficient represented a concatenation of partial effects that in their

TABLE 1-2
SIMPLE CORRELATIONS BETWEEN MONTHLY CHANGES IN INTEREST RATES

Period:	Fed funds rate with:	
	Ten-year Treasury	Thirty-year fixed-rate mortgage
2/1979 to 12/1987	0.40	0.58
1/1988 to 6/1996	0.34	0.40
7/1996 to 12/2001	0.03	0.13
2/2002 to 12/2006	−0.05	0.13
1/2007 to 6/2009	0.25	0.08

SOURCE: Federal Reserve Bank of St. Louis, FRED.

deep structure allowed the Fed some leeway. But perhaps not, or perhaps not in a manner that would have yielded predictable results.[11]

The Domestic Downturn

Housing market fundamentals softened starting in 2004 as an increasing number of buyers were priced out of the market and the Federal Reserve started raising short-term interest rates.[12] Meanwhile, economic growth slowed and the nation looked less favorably on immigration.

As a simple supply-and-demand framework dictates, a shift inward in the demand curve cuts the effective price of homes. But the housing market is not that simple. In particular, the effective price of houses has two components: the listed price of purchase and the price of financing that purchase. That is, home buyers care about a combination of both the sale price and the terms and standards on the mortgage.

Two problems forced most of the initial adjustment onto the funding, rather than the list price. First, the connection between commerce and finance in real estate had become so close and interconnected that both margins were seen to be in play by essentially the same actor—the builder linked to the real estate agent who was linked to the mortgage broker. Second, conversely, the bond between the loan officer who originated the mortgage and the final investor who held the security using that mortgage as collateral had weakened. The loan officer (mortgage broker) was compensated for the origination, not the final disposition, of the loan, creating a classic principal-agent problem.

Thus, in the face of a downturn in demand, a cut in the effective price of funding home purchases damped the reduction in the quantity of homes supplied. This involved approving too many mortgages with excessive leverage, cutting qualifying standards for those mortgages, steering borrowers to inappropriate loan products, and sometimes facilitating outright fraud. Prospective purchasers included unwitting victims of these aggressive practices and willing coconspirators who believed that double-digit capital gains would solve all their problems, even if their purchases were second houses or houses for quick resale.

In fact, there was only so much stretching that could be done in the financing of new houses before those excesses became evident. The first sign was when house-price appreciation stopped, seen by the peaking of the Case-Shiller national home-price index by spring 2006. Capital gains quickly faded and turned into losses. Loans made with poor prospects deteriorated in the downturn, as manifested in the poor payment performances on loans made in 2005 through 2007.

Resources that slowly enter an industry tend also to exit slowly. While builders slashed the construction of new homes, it was not at a sufficiently steep pace to prevent unsold inventories from accumulating. The contribution of real residential housing construction to GDP growth, which had averaged about a quarter of a percentage point from 1996 to 2005, turned negative in 2006. Since then, home building has been a drag on activity.

The end of the bubble also hit the resources and obligations of households. Table 1-3 presents an aggregate summary of the balance sheet of households (and nonprofit organizations) at the end of 2006 and changes from then to the first quarter of 2009. At the end of 2006, real estate represented about $24 trillion of household assets, or one-third of all assets and six-tenths of net worth. Real estate holdings were about $11 trillion greater than households' direct ownership of corporate equities and mutual fund shares. Claims on that real estate—home mortgages—totaled the single largest item on the liability side of household balance sheets. At the end of 2006, households had about $10 billion of mortgage debt outstanding,

TABLE 1-3
BALANCE SHEET OF HOUSEHOLDS AND NONPROFIT ORGANIZATIONS
(TRILLIONS OF DOLLARS)

	Out-standing at end of 2006	Change 2006 to 2009: Q1		Out-standing at end of 2006	Change 2006 to 2009: Q1
Total assets	75.6	−11.1	**Total liabilities**	13.4	0.7
of which:			*of which:*		
Real estate	24.2	−4.4	Home mortgages	9.9	0.6
Durable goods	3.9	0.3	Consumer credit	2.4	0.1
Equities and mutual fund shares	13.6	−5.1	**Net worth**	62.2	−11.8

SOURCE: Federal Reserve, Flow of Funds Accounts, B.100.

implying that total mortgage loans represented about 40 percent of the aggregate value of housing.

Capital losses on real estate since 2006 have had two material effects on aggregate economic activity. Households lost about $4.5 trillion of wealth in their homes, which has been compounded by the steeper slide in equity prices to bring net worth down $12 trillion. Households that are less wealthy consume less, and this paring off of consumption has been a drag on aggregate spending for some time. In addition, households have seen the equity component of their levered investment in real estate erode, with mortgages now representing 53 percent of aggregate real estate values. While this aggregate loan-to-value ratio seems conservative, the erosion of underwriting standards was uneven. Lax loan standards and price declines since the bubble burst have caused a minority of households' equity invest-ment in housing to evaporate. Many of those households have had payment difficulties or defaulted outright on their mortgages.

Those mortgages, which made home purchases possible, also served as the raw material for finance. Financial engineers diverted the promised payment streams from those mortgages into mortgage-backed securities and collateralized mortgage obligations. By way of comparison, Idaho potato farmers own, by law, the irrigation rights to the water in the top sixteen feet of Jackson Lake, Wyoming. As long as the water in Jackson Lake is at least sixteen feet at the start of the season, they will be able to exercise their rights fully. Similarly, investors in the top tranches of a mortgage-backed security would be repaid first, giving these securities an appearance of security— that is, as long as a severe drought did not come.

For holders of slices of pooled mortgage securities, a severe drought came. Losses on those mortgages reduced their value as collateral in mortgage-backed and collateralized-mortgage securities. Those losses punched holes through financial intermediaries' balance sheets. This led to a propagation of the initiating shock through markets both domestically and internationally.

What followed was a widespread reduction in risk taking. Financial institutions sought to conserve their capital in the face of losses on their mortgage-related securities, uncertainty about their own positions, and doubts about their counterparties. In that environment, credit became harder to get. This is a classic fallacy of composition. Firms' and individuals' efforts to repair balance sheets, by trying to sell their mortgage-related securities, drove down their prices and worsened the aggregate situation.

Magnification and Propagation Mechanisms

One surprise in this episode is that the initiating economic shock—the loss in home values associated with excesses in building and mortgage lending—appeared small and localized compared to the havoc wreaked on global markets. Four mechanisms contributed to the magnification and propagation of the shock, related to the similar US instruments held world-wide, the similar circumstances in several important countries, the linkages forged by trade, and competing demands on the shrinking pool of saving.

Losses on US Instruments Held Abroad. Because the United States had been financing current account deficits for some time, US mortgage-related risk had been dispersed across these financial institutions. Given that foreign entities faced the same sort of losses, their prospects similarly became clouded, and they and their counterparties withdrew from risk taking.

The fever chart of the banking system is the spread of eurodollar deposit rates over comparable maturity Treasury yields, shown in figure 1-10. The

FIGURE 1-10

SPREAD OF EURODOLLAR OVER TREASURY RATES

(BASIS POINTS)

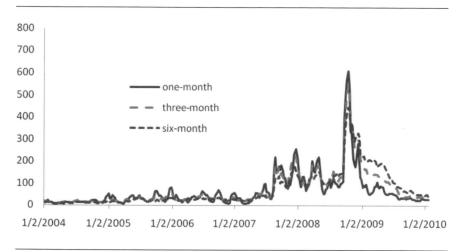

SOURCE: Federal Reserve.

spread compares two potential investments for a large, complex financial institution with an international presence. It can park excess funds in Treasury securities and earn a risk-free rate, or it can lend them to a competing, large, complex financial institution offshore, but in dollars, at the eurodollar deposit rate. The excess of the latter over the former is a measure of the perceived risk of such banking institutions or the relative premium attached to the safest of all investments—Treasury securities. It also measures the cost of bank-balance-sheet space, or how expensive it is to expand liabilities. From February 2004 to July 2007, these spreads averaged less than thirty basis points for the one-, three-, and six-month maturities. Since then, they have averaged at least one hundred basis points higher, indicating that balance-sheet space was expensive indeed. In such an environment, institutions were reluctant to support market activity, make new loans, or take advantage of arbitrage opportunities across markets.

Trading involves an act of faith—the faith that what is acquired can be resold or will return some form of value. Investors' faith in the value of securities supported by mortgage collateral was seriously shaken. Indeed, securities that were even tangentially related to the mortgage market were called into question. It became difficult for any one institution to discern how many dubious mortgage-backed securities it held and to determine whether its capital would provide a sufficient buffer should the value of those securities plummet in a general market rout. Without sufficient information to discriminate among institutions, investors stepped back from all of them. These changes in investors' participation in a market can have highly nonlinear effects on market liquidity due to the externalities generated by trading. In this environment, a small change in the willingness of investors to participate can cause a fairly sharp contraction in market activity.[13]

Note that the eurodollar panel of institutions used to survey the eurodollar deposit rate includes many large foreign institutions, so this premium on counterparty risk was not unique to US financial institutions. Indeed, the synchronized increase in spreads, decline in equity values, and contraction activity around the world was striking.

Similar Circumstances. The fundamental excesses of the US housing market were not unique to the United States. House prices were increasing at rapid rates in many countries, and foreign investors were flocking to those local markets. Reinhart and Reinhart (2008) show that a rapid step-up in capital inflows, which they termed a "capital flow bonanza," often goes hand-in-hand with rising housing and equity prices. They also show that when the bonanza fades away, those capital-market gains reverse. Playing out according to that script, Ireland, Iceland, Spain, New Zealand, and the United Kingdom were all among the countries that had outsized price appreciation followed by a crunching crash.

Figure 1-11 uses vintages of the IMF's *World Economic Outlook* to assess the consequences of the reduction in home prices for individual countries. The vertical axis plots the change from the growth forecast for GDP in 2008—made at the end of 2006—compared to the most recent growth estimate for that year for fifteen sample countries. That is, the axis measures how much the IMF staff marked down its forecast for growth over the preceding two and one-half years. The horizontal axis measures the average change in home prices from 2007 to 2008. As is evident, the more house prices have been marked down, the more so has the growth forecast.

FIGURE 1-11

HOUSE-PRICE CHANGES AND REVISIONS TO THE GDP GROWTH OUTLOOK

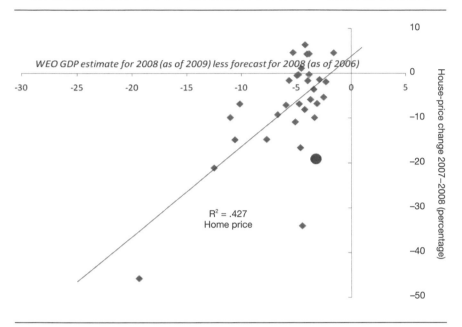

SOURCES: Author's calculations, IMF *World Economic Outlook*, and Global Property Registry.

It is also evident that the United States (marked with a dot) suffered from a lower downward growth revision given its home-price decline.

Transmission through Trade and Commodity Prices. Contracting income in many countries has shrunk world export demand, reflected both in declines in export volumes (as shown in figure 1-12) and falling commodity prices. The decline in world exports since its peak in July 2008 amounts to 42 percent, with some regions seeing their shipments fall by more than half.

As figure 1-13 shows, commodity prices similarly peaked in July 2008, and in aggregate declined about 35 percent by their trough in summer 2009. Included in that total were declines of 44 percent for primary metals and 30 percent for food. Not included in the nonfuel aggregate was the falloff in energy prices, which amounted to about 65 percent for crude oil. The decline in commodity prices has reversed about half of the run-up since 2001. This directly fed into the decline in export values for commodity

FIGURE 1-12

WORLD EXPORTS

(BILLIONS OF US DOLLARS)

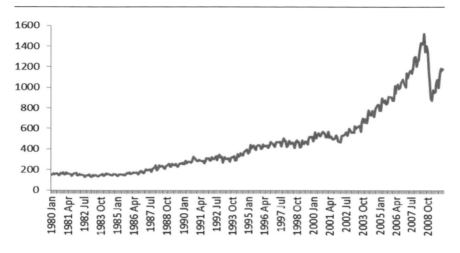

	Month of Peak	Month of Trough	Decline from Peak, Percentage
World	July 2008	Feb. 2009	–42%
Emerging and Developing Economies	July 2008	Feb. 2009	–45%
Africa	July 2008	Dec. 2008*	–30%
Commonwealth of Independent States and Mongolia	July 2008	Jan. 2009	–63%
Central and Eastern Europe	July 2008	Jan. 2009	–42%
Developing Asia	July 2008	Feb. 2009	–48%
Western Hemisphere	July 2008	Jan. 2009	–45%
Europe	July 2008	Jan. 2009	–53%

SOURCE: IMF, International Financial Statistics.
NOTE: *Trough is also most recent data.

producers and also exposed weaknesses in fiscal accounts for those countries where their leaders had thought the boom owed importantly to their own efforts and would last forever. This is a repeated error, as booms turn into busts (as explained in Boughton 1991 and Cuddington 1989). In many ways, the error was similar to that made in the early 1990s, a prior boomlet in capital flows analyzed by Calvo, Leiderman, and Reinhart (1993).

FIGURE 1-13
NONFUEL PRIMARY COMMODITY PRICES

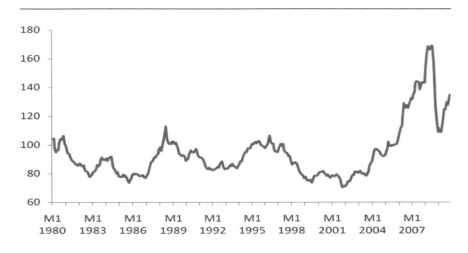

SOURCE: IMF, International Financial Statistics.
NOTE: Index, 2005 = 100.

As a report from the Inter-American Development Bank (2008) pointed out, fiscal and external accounts in emerging-market economies are not as healthy as they appeared on the surface, once accounting for the commodity-price boom.

A country-by-country depiction of the change in export values shows how crushing the force of restraint was for some nations. Figure 1-14 plots the twelve-month change in the value of exports ending in December 2008 for eighty-five countries. About one-quarter of that set registered declines of about 25 percent, with many of those including oil exporters. Only eleven countries in the sample showed an increase in exports in 2008.

Sudden Stops in Lending. No doubt, many excesses developed during the economic expansion. In the contraction that has followed, some of them have been revealed. When capital gains turn into capital losses, human frailties become more evident.

Declines in the value of US mortgage-related securities and equities directly lowered the wealth of investors. Readjusting relative portfolio

Figure 1-14
Export Values
(Change from 2007:12 to 2008:12, Percentage)

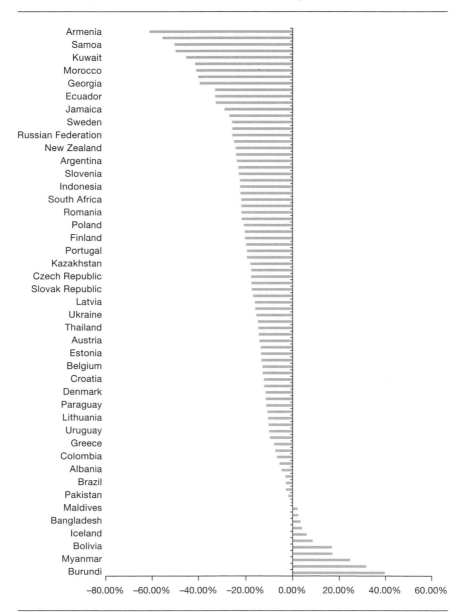

Source: IMF, *International Financial Statistics.*

shares given those losses led them to sell other assets, exacerbating the downward pressures in other markets. Less-wealthy investors were also more risk averse and prone to extrapolate the risk to all the national markets where they participated. This strained local financial markets, which crowded out domestic borrowers with good initial prospects.

For countries initially untouched by the US seizure, this sudden stop in lending, as in Calvo (1998), was the leading edge of restraint.[14] In current circumstances, large firms headquartered in Brazil, Colombia, and Mexico, to name a few, could no longer borrow on international markets or from multinational financial institutions. Shut out abroad, those firms returned home, where domestic financial institutions found them to be attractive and credit-worthy prospects. To some extent, domestic banks funded additional lending by attracting more deposits, exactly in the manner predicted by Kashyap, Rajan, and Stein (2002) that makes those institutions unique. But deposit creation lagged behind lending to big firms, so new lending to small and medium-size enterprises shrank. What followed was a silent credit crunch as domestic bank credit appeared to be robust even as net credit to the private sector (domestic plus foreign) contracted. The latter was more important to activity than the former, much to the chagrin of local officials who initially mistook strong domestic lending as evidence of "decoupling" with advanced economies.[15]

The Record of Policy Intervention

The tabulation of human frailty should not stop at the private sector. Actions by financial officials added to the losses, especially in 2008. This section analyzes three sets of policies—financial, fiscal, and monetary—with an emphasis on their international dimension and historical precedent.[16]

Financial Policies. The financial crisis first broke in summer 2007 when two hedge funds sponsored by Bear Stearns ran aground. US officials first sought private-sector solutions, consistent with the interpretation that there had been a massive withdrawal of liquidity from the market. That is, the prevailing view was that investors had become both extremely conscious and intolerant of risk.

As 2008 unfolded, officials still seemed wedded to that interpretation. As a result, policy interventions by the Treasury and the Federal Reserve were ambiguous as to the scale and scope of the protections offered. This created incentives for creditors and short sellers to test the limits of intervention. For the private sector, it lessened pressure on management to raise capital and address balance sheet problems. More generally, it lessened counterparty discipline, as lenders correctly anticipated that their obligations might be assumed by the US government. Those government actions opened important federal agencies to political pressure and tilted the political playing field toward intervention generally.

The possibility of intervention led investors to delay capital investments. That is, it deepened the capital hole. If the private sector became unwilling to fill the hole, the government would have to do so. Moreover, just as Treasury secretary Henry Paulson and Federal Reserve chairman Ben Bernanke were encouraging Congress to pass the Troubled Asset Relief Program legislation and justifying their takeover of the American International Group, confidence cratered. Brinkmanship is a problem inherent in bailouts. Political salesmanship does not always align with economic stewardship.

In 2009, US authorities acted more consistently, but in a way that encouraged financial institutions to delay the recognition of losses. The history of banking crises, as reviewed in Kaminsky and Reinhart (1999) and Frydl (1999), suggests that there are three stages in dealing with troubled financial institutions: (1) *When to recognize loss*, or when financial institutions write down the value of legacy assets sufficiently to reflect the bursting of the bubble; (2) *Who assumes loss*, or the combination of private- and public-sector support to fill holes on financial balance sheets associated with the recognition of loss; and (3) *What protections are given to investors*, or the assurances offered to the main holders of financial institutions' debt—depositors in the case of banks and shareholders in the case of mutual funds—so they do not flee the financial system. The timing of when, who, and what varies with each incident. Table 1-4 lists a few prominent examples and subjective interpretations of the steps to resolve the crisis.

The relatively laissez-faire approach of the Hoover administration in the initial stages of the Great Depression in the United States dictated that private losses be borne by the entities that had taken those exposures.[17] The problem, as was formalized by Diamond and Dybvig (1983) a half-century later, was that the private assumption of loss led depositors operating without a safety net to predict that being early in the queue to withdraw had a

TABLE 1-4
RESPONSES TO BANKING CRISES

	When to recognize loss?	Who assumes loss?	What protections are offered?
Hoover Depression (1929–32)	Quick	Private	None
Roosevelt Depression (1933–37)	—	Private/ Government	Government guarantee
Latin American Debt Crisis (1981–89)	Delayed	Private/ Government	Government swap of principal
US Thrift Crisis (1984–91)	Delayed	Private/ Government	Government guarantee
Japanese Banking Crisis (1981–89)	Delayed	Private/ Government	Government guarantee
Nordic Banking Crisis (1987–91)	Quick	Private/ Government	Government guarantee

SOURCE: Author.

decided advantage. When everyone does so, a run ensues. The resolution to that risk, found shortly after Franklin Roosevelt became president, was to insure deposits at a sufficiently high limit.

This solution, of course, has to balance protection from runs against augmentation of moral hazard, a problem that has bedeviled policymakers since 1933.[18] They do not always strike the right balance, as seen in the long lines snaked around the branches of the UK mortgage institution Northern Rock in 2007.[19] As is wont at a time of crisis, the pendulum subsequently swung to the other side to raise coverage significantly.[20]

The regulatory apparatus for financial institutions and impediments to international capital flows put in place during the Great Depression virtually eliminated financial crises for four decades, a startling fact documented in Reinhart and Rogoff (2009). As those controls were gradually lifted or circumvented, crises recurred. Policymakers, however, retained a lingering distaste for the private recognition of losses. Thus, when US money-center banks became technically insolvent, when Latin American countries began defaulting in 1981, when US thrifts went underwater following the bust in a regional real estate bubble in the mid-1980s, and when Japanese banks imploded near that same time, banks were allowed to delay the recognition of losses. This policy of forbearance, the argument runs, allows banks time to repair their balance sheets and lessens their need to tap markets for funding at a time when they are in disfavor.

Experience suggests otherwise. Forbearance permits bankers to delay adjustment, on the hope that the market for the troubled asset will recover. As a result of a regulatory decision, the stock of legacy assets at banks becomes more valuable sitting on the balance sheet than if resold. However, as Coase (1972) pointed out, the market-clearing price for a durable good depends on expectations of future as well as present sales. Trading in that asset class freezes.

By revealed preference, policymakers seem to have been willing to tolerate the cost of a dysfunctional market for the benefit of maintaining the perception that banks are still solvent on a regulatory-reporting basis. Economic performance mostly suffered.

Table 1-5 compares real GDP growth in major episodes of regulatory forbearance, listing real GDP growth in particular countries or regions relative to the world average, as is available in the IMF's *World Economic Outlook*. As is evident, Latin America (the Western Hemisphere in the IMF nomenclature) and Japan both had lost decades. They expanded about 1.75 percentage points slower than the world average during those stretches. The cumulative growth shortfall aggregated to 17 percent for the Western Hemisphere and 32 percent for Japan. The cost to the United States appeared smaller during the thrift crisis, but there were many other engines of recovery at that time.

An exception to this pattern was the handling of the Nordic banking crisis in the 1990s. Sweden and Norway forced a more immediate recognition of losses and, by nationalizing institutions, the government assumed part of the cost. The output loss was considerable, but short-lived. Of course, these small open economies had the benefit of a downturn asynchronous with the rest of the world and could rely more on exchange-rate depreciation as an engine of recovery.

US officials have opted for a policy of forbearance once again. The stress tests required of the leading nineteen firms emphasized opportunities for

TABLE 1-5
REAL GDP GROWTH RELATIVE TO THE WORLD, 1980 TO 2008
(PERCENTAGE POINTS)

	Western Hemi-sphere	Japan	United States	Norway	Sweden
"Lost" years	1981 to 1990	1992 to 2005	1984 to 1991	1987 to 1989	1991
Growth differential in lost years					
Average	−1.7	−2.2	−0.1	−3.1	−2.6
Cumulative	−17.1	−31.5	−0.5	−9.3	−2.6
Growth differential in all other years	0.3	0.0	−0.6	−0.1	−1.0

SOURCE: IMF, *World Economic Outlook,* April 2009.

flow profits rather than recognition of legacy losses.[21] Those financial institutions look better on the surface as described by regulatory accounting, but some of the assets they hold remain frozen on their balance sheets. Moreover, the United States, unlike the Nordic economies, is not a small, open economy, and one-sided flexibility in exchange rates does not always provide an effective safety valve. Against a backdrop of continued purchase of dollar assets by foreign, official entities, discussed earlier, and a flight to safety, the US dollar mostly appreciated through the early stages of the crisis.[22]

Fiscal Policy. What began as the subprime crisis in the United States during summer 2007 and morphed into a global financial crisis in the other advanced economies of the North—the United States, Ireland, the United Kingdom, Spain, Switzerland, and Japan—has led to unprecedented fiscal stimulus efforts worldwide. The North needed stimulus because banking crises are usually accompanied by severe and protracted recessions and rising unemployment. The South sought to stimulate domestic demand by fiscal means in the face of collapsing exports, as available financing from global capital markets dried up in a "sudden stop" as predicted by Calvo (1998).

FIGURE 1-15

EFFECT OF THE STIMULUS PLAN ON THE US FEDERAL BUDGET DEFICIT
(BILLIONS OF DOLLARS)

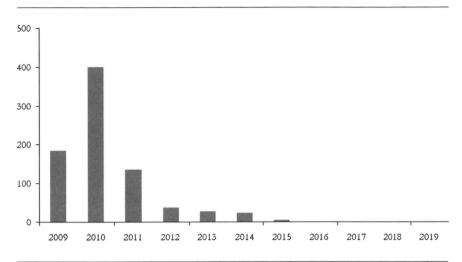

SOURCE: Congressional Budget Office, Letter to Speaker of the House Nancy Pelosi, February 23, 2009.

The US Congressional Budget Office (2009) tallied up the spending, taxation, and entitlement changes encompassed in the American Recovery and Reinvestment Act of 2009, shown in figure 1-15.[23] Noteworthy in that profile is the relatively slow spend-out rate. The government deficit widens a bit less than $200 billion in fiscal year (FY) 2009 and then more than twice that in FY 2010. The temporary impetus tails off through 2015.

Assessing the effects of this policy stimulus is, to understate matters, contentious. The empirical record is much more checkered than the standard multiplier exercises of textbooks (as discussed in Blanchard and Perotti 2002). Two aspects of the 2009 stimulus package run counter to making the bang-for-buck particularly high. First, as shown in table 1-6, support to state and local governments falls initially on areas where resources are already mostly used—health care and education. In such circumstances, additional demand falls more on the prices of those services rather than the quantities delivered. Second, many of the changes are programmatic and therefore unlikely to be rolled back when the temporary program ends.

TABLE 1-6

COMPOSITION OF STATE AND LOCAL GOVERNMENT RECOVERY ACT FUNDING
(SHARE OF THE TOTAL, PERCENTAGE)

	FY 2009	FY 2012
Health	64	1
Education and training	18	19
Transportation	8	30
Income security	6	17
Community development	6	16
Energy and environment	1	17

SOURCE: Government Accountability Office, "Recovery Act," April 2009, www.recovery.gov/sites/default/files/GAO-09-80+Recovery+Act.pdf.

Thus, market participants are more likely to view them as permanent additions to the baseline for federal involvement in the economy. As a result, capital markets are likely to price in higher borrowing rates in the future. As Blanchard (1981) showed, such "expectational" crowding out lessens the immediate efficacy of the policy.

If the adverse shock to the North had been a short-lived reduction in financing, as many observers believed at the time, emerging markets would have been well placed to cope with the shock. A combination of currency depreciation (now possible owing to more flexible exchange-rate arrangements) and some international reserve losses would seem to fit the bill. In addition, a short-lived fiscal response that entailed increasing government expenditures for a limited period of time did not seem to carry substantive risks to debt sustainability.

Fiscal stimulus packages in various guises and magnitudes found favor in both advanced and emerging economies. By January 2009, the *Global Economic Monitor,* published by the Institute for International Finance, detailed the packages either adopted or planned in about twenty advanced and emerging-market economies, including China, Korea, Mexico, and Saudi Arabia. Less than two months later, the list of countries had expanded to include Russia and Turkey, among others.[24] The IMF, both famous and infamous for advocating fiscal austerity packages in response to financial crises around the globe since its inception in 1945, began to advocate a "possible strategy whereby fiscal policy can foster the resumption of normal economic growth while maintaining public sector solvency."[25]

To be sure, avoiding the acute fiscal policy procyclicality that has plagued most emerging markets for decades is, indeed, progress. As Kaminsky, Reinhart, and Végh (2004) document, from 1965 to 2003 the most prevalent pattern in emerging markets during recessions (in contrast to their Organisation for Economic Co-operation and Development [OECD] counterparts) was sharp reductions in real discretionary fiscal spending. It is difficult to imagine that this would not help account for the greater volatility evident in emerging-market output.

Fashions are hard to resist, and it is now fashionable in much of the North to rely on fiscal engines for growth. As for emerging markets, however, boosting spending at a time in which revenues are contracting or, in many cases, collapsing for an uncertain period of time is a more complicated matter.[26] A few main risks arise:

Uncertainty about fiscal multipliers: Although there is little consensus in academic and policy circles as to point estimates, the discussion of fiscal multipliers in most OECD countries is at least informed by existing analytical and empirical studies. For emerging markets as a whole, however, it is fair to state that a comparable literature does not exist. Obviously, one can anticipate from the few reliable case studies that are available that the cross-country variation is bound to be substantial. Thus, any statement about fiscal multipliers for emerging markets (and developing countries) as a class has to be interpreted with care.

In that regard, especially timely work by Ilzetzki, Mendoza, and Végh (2009) calculates such multipliers for advanced high-income economies, emerging markets (middle income), and developing countries (low income) using quarterly data. Their analysis suggests that: (i) the fiscal multiplier on impact is larger for developing and emerging-market countries than for advanced high-income countries; (ii) the opposite is true for the peak multiplier; and (iii) the cumulative multipliers are far smaller for emerging markets than for advanced economies, as the positive impact of fiscal spending on GDP dies out fairly quickly.

Crowding out: Governments in advanced countries have put increased demands on available resources. As shown in table 1-7, government debt

TABLE 1-7

GOVERNMENT DEBT

(AS A SHARE OF NOMINAL GDP, PERCENTAGE)

	2007	2008
Euro Area	66.2	69.2
France	63.9	68.1
Germany	65.1	66.0
Italy	103.5	106.0
United Kingdom	44.2	52.0
Mexico	22.3	26.2
United States	36.5	40.8
India	5.2	5.3
Russian Federation	7.3	6.5
South Africa	25.0	23.0

SOURCE: IMF.

has increased in many major economies, including, when scaled to nominal GDP, an 8-percentage-point increase in the United Kingdom and a 4-percentage-point increase in the United States. Both advanced economies are at the lead, but they are not alone. Government debt as a share of GDP has increased 3 percentage points in the euro area. Still, those increases as yet fall short of the pattern found in Reinhart and Rogoff (2009). In a sample of twentieth-century financial crises in advanced and emerging-market economies, they found that the public debt increased 86 percent, on average, by the third year after the crisis. The direct costs of financial rescue, sluggish revenue associated with a poorly performing economy, and fiscal stimulus packages combine to put considerably higher demands on available saving.

This crowding out should mostly have consequences for the composition of aggregate demand, with relatively more coming from the government and less from the private sector. On net, as long as policy multipliers are positive in the short to medium run, economic activity should not have been set back as a consequence of an increased role for the government.

The illusory safety of domestic debt: The tilt in favor of domestic debt financing in recent years is by and large a welcome development, as it may help foster a domestic capital market. However, as Reinhart and Rogoff (2008) argue, domestic debt is not new. Though less well documented than comparable external defaults, domestic defaults have been numerous throughout history. Including domestic debt in the calculus helps explain why governments default on foreign debts at seemingly low levels of debt (see debt intolerance below) and why they resort to inflation as a means of reducing their debt burdens.

Debt intolerance: Historically, emerging-market defaults have taken place at levels of debt that appear to be safe and even conservative by advanced-economy standards. The defaults of Mexico in 1982 and Argentina in 2001 were not exceptions. Real exchange-rate depreciation typically accompanies a default, of course, as locals and foreign investors flee the currency. The fiscal "space" to implement ambitious stimulus plans in emerging markets is far more limited than in advanced economies—although policymakers in the latter may underestimate these constraints as well.

Monetary Policy. The Federal Reserve aggressively lowered its policy rate, seen as the dashed line in figure 1-16, over the course of 2008. The central bank significantly expanded the size of its balance sheet, as seen in the solid line, to more than $1 trillion by October 2008. That provision of liquidity drove the funds rate effectively to zero, even as the official target was initially still 1 percent. Despite the evidence both in quantities and prices, officials seemed reluctant to describe their policy as quantitative easing.[27] The Fed did not formally embrace quantitative easing for macroeconomic reasons until mid-December, when the Federal Open Market Committee officially pushed its target rate to 0–0.25 percent.[28]

Quantitative easing holds that the size and composition of the central bank's balance sheet influences financial markets and the economy over and beyond the level of the policy rate. One consequence of this definition is that policy does not necessarily run out of ammunition at the zero bound. That is, the central bank can still manipulate its balance sheet even as its policy rate is pinned at zero. This definition also implies that quantitative easing is not just about the level of reserves. The level of reserves is one portion of a central bank's balance sheet, but other liabilities and the size and composition of its assets can also influence the macroeconomy. In addition, this

FIGURE 1-16

TOTAL RESERVES AND THE FEDERAL FUNDS RATE

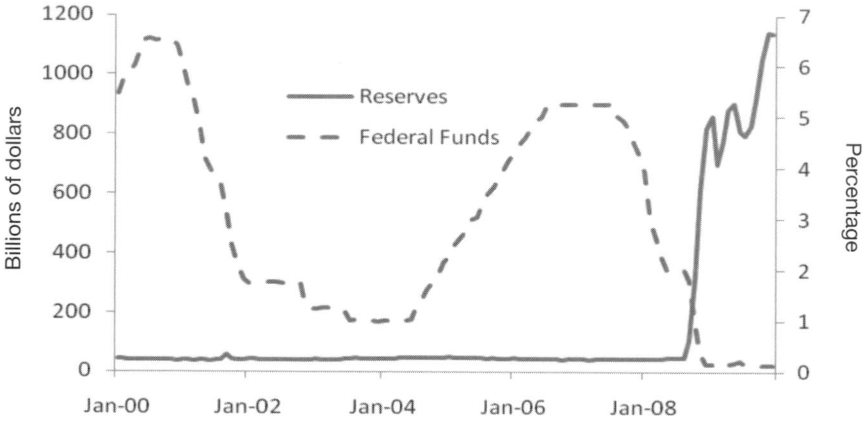

SOURCE: Federal Reserve Bank of St. Louis, FRED.

definition implies that quantitative easing can be undertaken at a nonzero-policy interest rate. This is relevant both for the central banks that have not already put the pedal fully to the metal, such as the European Central Bank, and for those that have but are now planning to unwind policy stimulus.

Quantitative easing potentially works on both sides of a central bank's balance sheet in the manner described by Bernanke and Reinhart (2004).

(1)   The large provision of reserves may induce banks to make use of idle balances, which is the traditional **money-multiplier** effect. Even as the policy rate is pushed to zero, reserves can expand, potentially massively, providing banks the wherewithal to support deposit creation, if they are so inclined.

(2)   The overprovision of reserves also could help convince market participants that the policy interest rate will be low for a long time. This is known as the **policy duration** effect. This simply recognizes that the bigger the balance sheet, the longer it will likely take to shrink (in the manner described by Auerbach and Obstfeld, 2004).

(3) On the asset side, the accumulation of portfolio holdings might influence relative spreads and the function of markets, which is an **asset substitution** effect (in the manner of Tobin 1970).

(4) A central bank holding more assets—particularly those that have higher-than-typical returns, and importantly above the remuneration on deposits—should generate additional income. This central bank profit may encourage the government to spend more or to cut taxes, which is known as **creating fiscal space**.

When considering the risks of quantitative easing, it is important to remember that the tools that allow the expansion of the central bank's balance sheet are not inherently asymmetric. Mechanically, the central bank can shrink its balance sheet just as fast as it was expanded. Rather, the question is about the willingness of the central bank to be symmetrically aggressive, not the ability. In that regard, quantitative easing is probably most effective when there is a well-defined exit strategy. The anchoring of inflation expectations in the long run at an appropriate level gives policymakers leeway to be aggressive in the short run.

Some comfort can be taken from the fact that the Bank of Japan was able to unwind its balance sheet relatively quickly. In five remarkable months in 2006, the Bank of Japan shrank total assets by about a fifth. The contraction came mostly from its portfolio of government securities. The short average maturity of that portfolio allowed the asset stock to contract by merely rolling off maturing obligations.

While this has been done before, there are four reasons to be concerned about the Federal Reserve's willingness to head for the exit. First, policymakers might be unwilling to test the resilience of markets. They might easily convince themselves that the improvement in markets and the economy is due to the massive size of the Federal Reserve balance sheet. While financial markets and the economy might be better, they might not be strong enough to withstand the removal of that accommodation. A regular tendency over time and across countries is for policy rates to move asymmetrically. Policy rates tend to decline quickly and increase slowly. This is referred to as going up by the escalator and down by the elevator.[29] If policy rates are asymmetric even though there is no obvious cost to adjustment, we should not be surprised to find that changes in the balance sheet are similarly asymmetric.

Second, some long-lived assets on the Federal Reserve balance sheet might no longer have markets when the time comes for the Fed to sell them. This mostly holds for the assets in the special purpose vehicles and the potential purchase of legacy securities as part of the Treasury's rescue plan.[30]

Third, the Treasury has funded a portion of some Fed programs by providing a first-loss tranche. If the Treasury was present at the creation, does it also have to be amenable at the closure?

Fourth, political pressures might be intense. The Fed has been able to play a forceful role in affecting private credit markets. Congress might view this as the purview of fiscal policy and be more willing to interfere with those decisions going forward.

There has been significant international cooperation—both in providing central banks swap lines and providing support to financial institutions more generally. As shown in table 1-8, for instance, the more than doubling of the Federal Reserve's balance sheet has been surpassed by the Bank of England. Significant increases have also occurred in the euro area and in some emerging-market economies.

Conclusion

The exit from governmental entanglements of 2007–09 was difficult. Many advanced economies have significant ownership positions in large financial firms. Indeed, government ownership has found its way into significant nonfinancial firms as well; witness the ownership stake in the US automakers. Such governmental ownership has inherent conflicts. Should officials be concerned about the financial health of the firms they own, or the constituents those firms employ? The record from emerging-market economies is quite distinct. Governmental ownership implies governmental losses. Assets held by the government decline in value over time, as the government considers more than maximizing profits in running those firms.

The Federal Reserve has taken direct responsibility for the support of firms and markets in ways it has never done before. Moving back to the private assumption of loss and opportunity for profit may take some time. How quickly that is engineered will affect many aspects of private-sector risk taking and economic growth. It is not evident that public-sector protections are now in place to ease that transition.

TABLE 1-8
CENTRAL BANK ASSETS
(CHANGE OVER CORRESPONDING PERIOD OF PREVIOUS YEAR, PERCENTAGE)

	2007	2008	2009Q1
Argentina	29	13	9
Australia	−14	82	33
Brazil	43	37	35
Canada	10	47	
China, P.R.: Mainland	38	23	16
Euro Area	32	57	48
India	32	11	8
Indonesia	18	4	12
Japan	−2	8	
Korea, Republic of	5	2	15
Mexico	11	34	28
Russian Federation	48	37	37
Saudi Arabia	36	45	18
South Africa	22	36	16
Turkey	−5	38	28
United Kingdom	−19	147	220
United States	5	147	132

SOURCE: IMF.

References

Akerlof, George A., and Robert J. Shiller. 2009. *Animal Spirits*. Princeton, NJ: Princeton University Press.

Auerbach, Alan J., and Maurice Obstfeld. 2004. "Monetary and Fiscal Remedies for Deflation." *American Economic Review* 94 (2): 71–75.

Bank for International Settlements. 2009. *79th Annual Report*. Basel, CH: Bank for International Settlements.

Bernanke, Ben S. 2005. "The Global Saving Glut and the US Current Account Deficit." Sandridge Lecture, Virginia Association of Economics.

Bernanke, Ben, and Vincent Reinhart. 2004. "Conducting Monetary Policy at Very Low Short-Term Interest Rates," *American Economic Review,* 94(2): 85–90.

Blanchard, Olivier J. 1981. "Output, the Stock Market, and Interest Rates." *American Economic Review* 71 (March): 132–43.

Blanchard, Olivier J., and Roberto Perotti. 2002. "An Empirical Characterization of the Dynamic Effects of Changes in Government Spending and Taxes on Output." *Quarterly Journal of Economics* 117 (November): 1329–68.

Boughton, James. 1991. "Commodity and Manufactures Prices in the Long Run." International Monetary Fund Working Paper No. 91/47 (May).

Calvo, Guillermo A. 1998. "Capital Flows and Capital-Market Crises: The Simple Economics of Sudden Stops." *Journal of Applied Economics* 1, no. 1: 35–54.

Calvo, Guillermo A., Alejandro Izquierdo, and L. F. Mejia. 2004. "On the Empirics of Sudden Stops: The Relevance of Balance Sheet Effects." NBER Working Paper 10520.

Calvo, Guillermo A., Leonardo Leiderman, and Carmen M. Reinhart. 1993. "Capital Inflows and Real Exchange Rate Appreciation in Latin America: The Role of External Factors." *IMF Staff Papers* 40, no. 1 (March): 108–151.

Carroll, Christopher, and Olivier Jeanne. 2008. "A Tractable Model of Precautionary Reserves, Net Foreign Assets, or Sovereign Wealth Funds." NBER Working Paper 15228.

Case, Karl E., and Robert J. Shiller. 1989. "The Efficiency of the Market for Single-Family Homes." *American Economic Review* 79, no. 1 (March): 125–37.

Coase, Ronald H. 1972. "Durability and Monopoly." *Journal of Law and Economics* 15, no. 1 (April): 143–49.

Congressional Budget Office. 2009. "Estimated Impact on the Deficit of Three Alternative Policy Scenarios Specified by Speaker Pelosi and Chairman Spratt." Feb 23.

Cottarelli, Carlo. 2009. "Paying the Piper." *Finance and Development* 46, no. 1 (March).

Cuddington, John. 1989. "Commodity Export Booms in Developing Countries." *World Bank Research Observer* 4: 143–165.

Diamond, Douglas W., and Philip H. Dybvig. 1983. "Bank Runs, Deposit Insurance, and Liquidity." *Journal of Political Economy* 91: 401–419.

Dooley, Michael, and Peter Garber. 2005. "Is It 1958 or 1968? Three Notes on the Longevity of the Revived Bretton Woods System." Brookings Papers on Economic Activity.

Frankel, Jeffrey. 2007. "Getting Carried Away: How the Carry Trade and Its Potential Unwinding Can Explain Movements in International Financial Markets." Mimeograph, Harvard University, November.

Frydl, Edward J. 1999. "The Length and Cost of Banking Crises." International Monetary Fund Working Paper (March).

Ilzetzki, Ethan, Enrique Mendoza, and Carlos Végh. 2009. "How Big (Small?) Are Fiscal Multipliers?" Mimeograph, University of Maryland College Park.

Institute for International Finance. 2009. *Global Economic Monitor*. Washington, DC: Institute for International Finance, January.

Inter-American Development Bank. 2008. *All That Glitters May Not Be Gold: Assessing Latin America's Recent Macroeconomic Performance*. Washington, DC: Inter-American Development Bank, March.

Kaminsky, Graciela L., and Carmen M. Reinhart. 1999. "The Twin Crises: The Causes of Banking and Balance-of-Payments Problems." *American Economic Review* 89, no. 3: 473–500.

Kaminsky, Graciela L., Carmen M. Reinhart, and Carlos A.Végh. 2004. "When It Rains, It Pours: Procyclical Capital Flows and Policies." In *NBER Macroeconomics Annual 2004*, edited by Mark Gertler and Kenneth S. Rogoff, 11–53. Cambridge, MA: MIT Press.

Kane, Edward J. 1985. *The Gathering Crisis in Federal Deposit Insurance*. Cambridge, MA: MIT Press.

Kashyap, Anil K., Raghuram Rajan, and Jeremy C. Stein. 2002. "Banks as Liquidity Providers: An Explanation for the Coexistence of Lending and Deposit-Taking." *Journal of Finance* 57, no. 1 (February): 33–73.

Kearl, James. 1979. "Inflation, Mortgages, and Housing." *Journal of Political Economy* 87: 1115–38.

Kindleberger, Charles P. 1989. *Manias, Panics, and Crashes: A History of Financial Crises*. New York: Basic Books.

Mendoza, Enrique G., and Marco E. Terrones. 2008. "An Anatomy of Credit Booms: Evidence from Macro Aggregates and Micro Data." National Bureau of Economic Research Working Paper 14049. May. http://www.nber.org/papers/w14049.

Obstfeld, Maurice, and Kenneth Rogoff. 2000. "Perspectives on OECD Capital Market Integration: Implications for US Current Account Adjustment." In *Global Economic Integration: Opportunities and Challenges*. Federal Reserve Bank of Kansas City, 169–208.

Prasad, Eswar, and Isaac Sorkin. 2009. "Assessing the G-20 Stimulus Plans: A Deeper Look." Mimeograph. Washington, DC: Brookings Institution, March.

Reinhart, Carmen M., and Vincent R. Reinhart. 2008. "Is the US Too Big to Fail?" VoxEU.org, November.

Reinhart, Carmen M., and Kenneth S. Rogoff. 2008. "The Forgotten History of Domestic Debt." National Bureau of Economic Research Working Paper 13946. April.

———. 2009. *This Time Is Different: Eight Centuries of Financial Folly*. Princeton, NJ: Princeton University Press.

Reinhart, Vincent R., and Brian P. Sack. 2000. "The Economic Consequences of Disappearing Government Debt." *Brookings Papers on Economic Activity* no. 2: 163–220.

Shiller, Robert J. 1993. *Macro Markets*. Oxford, UK: Clarendon Press.

Shlaes, Amity. 2007. *The Forgotten Man: A New History of the Great Depression*. New York: HarperCollins.

Swagel, Phillip. 2009. "The Financial Crisis: An Inside View." *Brookings Papers on Economic Activity*, Spring.

Taylor, John B. 2009. *Getting Off Track: How Government Actions and Interventions Caused, Prolonged, and Worsened the Financial Crisis.* Stanford, CA: Hoover Institution Press.

Tobin, James. 1970. "A General Equilibrium Approach to Monetary Theory." *Journal of Money, Credit and Banking* 2 (November): 461–72.

Notes

Valuable research assistance provided by Meagan Berry, Greg Howard, and Adam Paul.

1. Thinkexist.com, "John Fitzgerald Kennedy Quotes," http://thinkexist.com/quotation/victory_has_a_thousand_fathers-but_defeat_is_an/210525.html (accessed April 17, 2012).

2. As in Calvo (1998).

3. Kearl (1979) used exactly that differential adjustment speed to generate a model of overshooting in home prices.

4. Akerlof and Shiller (2009) build a compelling case that the road less traveled of extrapolation and shifting waves of confidence help to explain events. A rereading of Kindleberger (1989) teaches the same lesson.

5. Robert Shiller (1993) addressed this issue in terms of institutional design.

6. As discussed, for instance, in Obstfeld and Rogoff (2000).

7. See the discussion of Dooley and Garber (2005). This argument has come in different guises, including as the "global saving glut," as put forward by then–Fed governor Ben Bernanke (2005).

8. The rationality of that reserve accumulation is explored in Carroll and Jeanne (2008).

9. That holds for the portion of reserves for which currency composition can be attributed. The unattributed portion is probably even more heavily concentrated in dollars. See International Monetary Fund, "Currency Composition of Official Foreign Exchange Reserves (COFER)," www.imf.org/external/np/sta/cofer/eng/index.htm.

10. Among the prominent critics is Taylor (2009) and analysts at the Bank for International Settlements (2009).

11. That said, housing activity linked to short-term interest rates, namely adjustable-rate financing, was more amenable to Fed influence over this period. In that regard, the issue might more appropriately be couched in terms of the Fed's gradual adjustment of its policy rate starting in 2004. Policy gradualism created intertemporal bargains that benefited short-term funding. An additional effect of policy gradualism may have been to encourage financial strategies reliant on low short-term interest rates—the "carry trades" described in Frankel (2007).

12. As noted earlier, the restraint from the Fed was felt exclusively on the short end of the interest-rate structure. Given the prevalence of adjustable-rate financing, this must have imparted some drag on the housing market.

13. A simple model highlighting the self-referencing nature of liquidity is given in Reinhart and Sack (2000).

14. See also Calvo, Izquierdo, and Mejia (2004).

15. Mendoza and Terrones (2008) provide macro and micro evidence on the importance of a credit channel in emerging-market economies.

16. Swagel (2009) gives the Treasury interpretation of this sequence of events.

17. That President Hoover was willing to drift from these principles is a theme of Shlaes (2007).

18. Kane (1985) addresses these costs and benefits.

19. The long queue seems rational, since at the time the United Kingdom covered only 100 percent of the first £2,000 and 90 percent of the next £33,000 of deposits.

20. The sequence sheds light on the difficulties in conducting policy with open capital markets. The government of Ireland first offered virtually unlimited coverage as its international banks faced the possibility of a run. But the allure of that insurance, even if given by a small country relative to the size of its obligations, threatened a tsunami of deposit flows away from other European Union countries to the protected locale. Other countries followed suit in an example of policy emulation, not policy coordination.

21. A description of the "Supervisory Capital Assessment Program" can be found at www.treasury.gov/press-center/press-releases/Pages/tg121.aspx

22. Reinhart and Reinhart (2008c) discuss this flight to safety.

23. See Congressional Budget Office, Letter to Senate Majority Letter Harry Reid, February 11, 2009, www.cbo.gov/sites/default/files/cbofiles/ftpdocs/99xx/doc9984/hr1senatepassed.pdf.

24. See Prasad and Sorkin (2009).

25. See Cottarelli in the IMF's March 2009 *Finance and Development* issue.

26. This is not intended to underestimate the difficulty and (usually) controversy of undertaking any kind of change in fiscal policy in the advanced economies.

27. Note, for instance, that Chairman Bernanke's testimony on monetary policy and the outlook on October 20, 2008, was silent on the level of reserves and the federal funds rate. See Board of Governors of the Federal Reserve System, "Economic Outlook and Financial Markets" (testimony before the Committee on the Budget, US House of Representatives, October 20, 2008), www.federalreserve.gov/newsevents/testimony/bernanke20081020a.htm (accessed April 17, 2012).

28. This is noted in the statement of the Federal Open Market Committee at the conclusion of its year-end meeting. See Board of Governors of the Federal Reserve System, press release, December 16, 2008, www.federalreserve.gov/newsevents/press/monetary/20081216b.htm (accessed April 17, 2012).

29. See, for example, Donald L. Kohn, "Success and Failure of Monetary Policy since the 1950s" (speech, conference to mark the fiftieth anniversary of the Deutsche Bundesbank, Frankfurt, Germany, September 21, 2007), www.federalreserve.gov/newsevents/speech/kohn20070921a.htm

30. In that regard, the Fed has already reached an accord with the Treasury for it to assume those special purpose vehicle assets when the time comes.

PART I

Markets React

2

An Alliance of Convenience

Christopher Whalen

October 2009

For the better part of a decade, many smart, talented people in the worlds of finance and economics have been struggling to describe the causes of the financial crisis and solutions. I witnessed such a debate recently at the international banking conference sponsored by the Federal Reserve Bank of Chicago. It is fair to say that the representatives from Europe, Asia, and the Americas continue to have differing views of the crisis and how to address it; more regulation or less, more capital or less, and whether markets should be reregulated.

Far from being dismayed by such disparity of views, I am encouraged by this difference of opinion and I hope that the debate intensifies in coming months. To recall the words of Alfred Sloan, only by sharpening our differences can we understand complex problems and understand those distinctions that matter and those that do not. But as we build a narrative to understand the crisis, we seem to be converging on one view of the causes of the financial bubble and thereby ignoring other perspectives and views that might be instructive.

In his book *The Black Swan,* Nassim Taleb warns us that the media, and particularly condensed versions of reality such as television, force us into an oversimplified view of the world. As social creatures, we tend to use narrative to describe and understand complexity. We speak and write and discuss. Gradually we distill our impressions, and these views merge together into the collective understanding, the "official" story.

But just as bubbles are probably not a good technical metaphor to describe financial crises,[1] we need to beware the tendency to simplify and categorize complex events when it comes to public policy for our financial institutions and markets. Americans have a wonderful tendency to look at public policy from a vertical perspective, in silos that suggest we can somehow isolate monetary policy and bank supervision and fiscal policy into neat, separate little boxes that are never affected or disturbed by one another. In particular, this comes to mind when we hear economists talk about foreign capital inflows as an externality. Those fiat paper dollars belong to us. We printed them and of course they are returning home in search of at least a nominal return. That is why we have problems such as mortgage-market bubbles and a surfeit of capital inflows, then a sudden outflow of these same pools of credit. In a fiat money system, after all, there is no "money" in a classical sense, merely credit. These large flows of fiat paper dollars, I submit, explain the increasingly manic behavior of markets, investors, and large banks over the past decade as true investment opportunities are increasingly outnumbered by speculation.

America's addiction to debt and inflationary monetary policy makes it difficult for us to address more basic structural problems in our economy. This is especially true so long as the rest of the world is willing to allow the United States to retain a global monopoly on dollars as the primary means of exchange and as a short-term store of value. But I believe that to achieve a true understanding of the crisis, we must step back and take a political perspective.

The evolution of the United States from a democratic republic into a more statist, corporate formulation like the states of Europe and Asia makes concepts such as too big to fail (TBTF) and systemic risk viable. The migration of the United States from a society based on individual liberty, work, and responsibility to a society where a largely corporate and socialist perspective holds sway is changing the way we look at our financial and monetary systems. Because of the huge and, some would say, illegal subsidies provided to Wall Street firms during the early part of the crisis, particularly in cases such as the rescue of American International Group,[2] the American electorate is engaged in an intense, sometimes angry, debate about financial policy and government.

This debate is also intense among the bank-regulatory community, with Federal Deposit Insurance Corporation (FDIC) chair Sheila Bair, the FDIC and state regulators, and smaller banks supporting a traditional if somewhat legalistic American view of banks on issues like insolvency and resolution, on the one hand. On the other hand, the large banks, the Federal Reserve Board, Treasury, and the White House represent the internationalist tendency and, like the leaders of the European Union (EU), advocate a socialist and statist perspective where banks are TBTF and under-the-table subsidies to well-connected institutions are encouraged. Whereas in the 1800s, New York banks advocated hard money and sound banks, and the inflationists were among the agrarian populist ranks, today it is Washington, Paris, and Berlin, among the largest dealer banks and their political allies, that advocate inflation and public-sector debt.

The Fed and Treasury seem to know nothing about American values when it comes to insolvency or bank safety and soundness. Our founders embedded bankruptcy in the Constitution not out of generosity, but because they knew that prompt resolution and liquidation of claims benefited all of society. The internationalist set, like their counterparts in Europe and Japan, talk of the ill effects of resolving zombie banks through traditional bankruptcy, but they fail to notice the benefits with equal concern. If we do not have losers as well as winners, then we shall have neither. For every loser at Lehman Brothers and Washington Mutual, there were winners at JPMorgan Chase and Barclays PLC, which bought the assets of the failed companies for pennies on the dollar and absorbed thousands of valuable employees.

The internationalists at the Fed and Treasury prefer instead to align themselves with foreign countries whose governments are predominantly socialist in economic orientation and authoritarian politically. These politicians and their economists prefer to pick "losers as winners," to paraphrase my friend Bob Feinberg.[3] Look at the situation in Germany, where the political leadership refused even to acknowledge the depth of the crisis in the state or private banking sector. Germany is a case study illustrating the corruption and incompetence that prevails when the political class is allowed to take unilateral control over all financial institutions and markets.[4]

It is both fascinating and troubling to watch members of the Fed staff being seduced by the siren song of political expediency on issues such as systemic risk, a political concept that has no place in a serious discussion of finance. Certain banks, say Fed and Treasury officials, are TBTF. But just as true finance is about the arithmetic certainty of market prices and cash flow rather than speculative models, Fed officials seem to confuse safety and soundness in a financial sense with pleasing the political class that inhabits both major political parties in Washington.

Fed officials recite the mantra about how Lehman Brothers should not have been allowed to fail and large banks are too connected globally to be subject to traditional resolutions, as in the failures of both Lehman and Washington Mutual. When I point out to these same Fed officials that Lehman had been for sale, unsuccessfully, for a year, I hear only silence. When I note that Harvey Miller, working as a bankruptcy and Securities Investor Protection Corporation trustee, and the good people of the Southern District of New York did a fine job handling the Lehman insolvency, there is likewise only silence from the TBTF advocates. Instead of being used as an excuse for inaction and delay, the insolvency of Lehman Brothers and Washington Mutual should be held up as examples of the American legal system functioning well.

When officials at the Fed and Treasury are challenged about TBTF and systemic risk, they point out that using bankruptcy to resolve complex institutions is too damaging to confidence. Mr. Reinhart mentions in his introduction that avoiding damage to confidence is a top-level priority for policymakers. But if we have such a rule, then we cannot have a true market system. Markets must be allowed to go from exuberance to terror in order to have true price discovery and a free and democratic society. Investors, bank managers, and politicians can only be held accountable if failure is allowed to occur. If we allow government to legislate confidence through the imposition of systemic-risk regulators and rules such as TBTF, then we will not be a free society for much longer.

To see where the United States is headed by embracing concepts such as systemic risk and TBTF, look at the European Union, where whole countries have lost their private banking sector, where there is no private capital formation to create new banks, and where the state has monopolized many areas of personal and commercial finance. In 2008, there were more *de novo* banks created in the state of Texas than in the entire EU. By not allowing failure and insolvency for even the largest banks and companies in the United States, we deprive our citizens of future opportunity.

It should come as no surprise that most of the damage done to EU banks in the latest speculative cycle is found among state-sector banks. Claims by

EU politicians that regulation effectively mitigates financial risk are belied by the facts. EU politicians and bureaucrats may have regulated away bad acts and freedom of choice for private investors, but that only means that the misbehavior has migrated to the public sector and benefits the entrenched political elites. We see the same pattern now in the United States.

Let us turn now to Fed policy—whether the Fed can be both an effective safety-and-soundness regulator and a monetary authority, especially given the corporatist political evolution already mentioned. There are three significant groupings of political power flows in the United States today:

First, we have a central bank that manages a global fiat dollar system based on a currency unit that is not convertible into specie or commodities. The Fed enables the issuance of dollar debt by the Treasury and imposes no effective policy restraint or check to balance US fiscal policy. In fact, since the October 1987 crisis, the Fed has never said no to Congress or the markets in terms of liquidity or collateral. It has only been a matter of price. When was the last time we had a Fed chair willing to say no to politicians in the White House or Congress? Paul Volcker? I suggest that it has been far too long.

Second, we have a corrupt, entrenched Congress that equates tax revenues with the proceeds of debt. All fiat paper dollars are one and the same to Congress, which believes that the borrowing capacity of the United States is infinite. There is no effective limit on spending to keep the electorate mollified and the entrenched political class in power. The Fed enables the spending habit of the Congress and whatever administration occupies the White House.

Some supporters of former Fed chair Alan Greenspan like to argue that no Fed chair could have stopped the party's work in housing, and that no Fed chair could say tough things to Capitol Hill about housing policy or public spending. However, tough-talking Fed governors are precisely what we need. If the heads of independent agencies are not ready to lose their jobs every day and willing to take tough policy stands on equally tough issues, then we need new leaders. Bair at the FDIC is an example of a public servant who understands that part of her job is to offer advice to Congress and the White House, not to be a creature of politics or special interests.

Third, we have the dealer community, especially the primary dealers of US government securities, who have a special relationship with the Fed and

Treasury, most recently by placing a former Wall Street chieftain as secretary of the Treasury. Many of these banks created the trillions of dollars in toxic waste that has crippled our financial system and were subsequently bailed out by the extraordinary actions taken by Federal Reserve Bank of New York president Timothy Geithner and the Fed's Board of Governors starting in 2008.

These large dealers, such as JPMorgan, Goldman Sachs, Wells Fargo, Morgan Stanley, and Citigroup, enable the Treasury to sell debt and thereby keep the US fiat dollar system stable for another day. These large, TBTF banks were also the mechanism through which the Fed executed monetary policy, until the Federal Reserve itself grew operationally into a *de facto* primary dealer in its own right, merging fiscal and monetary policy explicitly.[5]

To boost the profitability of these TBTF dealer banks, the Fed and Congress encouraged the creation of opaque, unregulated over-the-counter (OTC) markets for derivatives and complex assets. The growth of OTC markets is a retrograde development in historical terms and again illustrates the tendency of the Fed and Treasury, Congress, and large banks to take an anti-American view of issues like market structure, transparency, and solvency. They encourage instruments of fraud-like OTC derivatives and private placements, while the FDIC, state regulators, and smaller banks tend to oppose such innovations. By allowing the creation of derivatives for which there was no basis, the Fed enabled some of the worst acts by the dealer community such as collateralized debt obligations that led to the 2007 financial crisis.

OTC markets for derivatives and structure assets have been the primary source of systemic risk over the past decade and have contributed the lion's share of losses sustained by banks and the taxpayers of industrial nations. Indeed, without the active support of Congress and the Fed for "innovations" such as OTC and opaque, unregistered, complex structured securities, the current crisis might never have occurred. The alien nature of "dark pools" and closed, bilateral market structures such as OTC go against the most basic American principles of transparency and fairness.

The analog to the political checks and balances revered in the history books is a public, open-outcry market. Whether virtual or physical, an open market structure is essential for having true confidence in markets. When markets slip back into retrograde formulations like OTC, the basis of American markets, namely openness and fairness, is eroded. If our OTC markets are deliberately opaque, unfair, and deceptive, then can we reasonably hope that our financial institutions and markets will be stable?[6]

Our spendthrift government, the Federal Reserve System, and the TBTF banks together now comprise the paramount political tendency in the United States. This tripartite "alliance of convenience" fits beautifully into the corporatist mold that is America in the twenty-first century—but only viewed by the elites in cities like New York and Washington. Many Americans of all political descriptions oppose this corrupt and unaccountable political formulation.

What separates the United States from the rest of the world is our at least theoretical devotion to individual liberty and free markets. Until we break the alliance of convenience among Congress, the Fed, and the large, TBTF banks and force our public officials to embrace core American values regarding transparency, insolvency, and accountability, we will not find a way out of the crisis. In many ways, what separates the popular view and the views of our political elite has been turned on its head compared with a century ago, but this does not mean that the debate and resulting political competition for ideas will be any less intense.

Notes

This commentary is based on remarks from the October 9, 2009, conference held at AEI and is part of the "No Way Out: Government Response to the Financial Crisis" series organized by Vincent R. Reinhart, resident scholar at the American Enterprise Institute. The author wishes to thank Mr. Reinhart and AEI for the invitation to contribute to this discussion and Greg Ip of The Economist and Angel Ubide of Tudor Corporation for their comments.

1. At Institutional Risk Analytics, we tend to favor physical models such as entropy to describe the movement of markets, as opposed to the statistical distributions that dominate mainstream financial economics.

2. The payments made to the over-the-counter dealer counterparties of American International Group by the Federal Reserve Bank of New York are arguably illegal and may yet be the subject of inquiry in the political and legal arenas.

3. See "All about Picking Losers as Winners: Interview with Bob Feinberg," The Institutional Risk Analyst, August 5, 2009.

4. See "Germany's Subprime Crisis: Interview with Achim Dubel," The Institutional Risk Analyst, May 27, 2009.

5. In the present crisis, the Federal Reserve Bank of New York and other reserve banks have changed dramatically and resumed a direct role as a provider of credit in the private financial markets, in many cases bypassing the dealer banks. Perhaps those beautiful teller windows in the lobby of the Federal Reserve Bank of New York will once again be used by individuals when the next deflationary phase of the financial crisis becomes fully apparent.

6. See *Statement by Christopher Whalen, Before the Senate Committee on Banking Housing and Urban Affairs, Subcommittee on Securities, Insurance, and Investment*, 110th Cong. (June 22, 2009), www.rcwhalen.com/pdf/StatementbyChristopherWhalen_SBC_062209.pdf (accessed April 17, 2012).

3

Paradigm Lost:
A Discussion of "No Way Out"

Angel Ubide

October 2009

Vincent Reinhart's paper makes a critical point early in the introduction: the narrative of this crisis—the conclusions that the economics profession draws regarding the causes and the management of the crisis—will be its most permanent impact over the global economy, above and beyond the sharp recession it has created, the increase in unemployment, and the drastic change in the financial sector landscape. This narrative will define the policy changes that will ensue and thus the way markets and economies will operate over the next decades.

Therefore, this discussion will focus on the genesis of the crisis, the crisis itself, and the policy response. The debate in the United States centers on failures in US supervision and regulation and Wall Street idiosyncrasies. The debate in Europe and Asia centers more on global imbalances and the failures of monetary policy. Either all these views are right at the same time, or they are all probably wrong, or at least incomplete.

Therefore, we will cut across some of these issues and discuss some general conclusions.[1] First of all, this crisis should be reframed as a credit crisis, not a housing crisis or banking crisis. This credit crisis is defined by excess leverage in the global economy, which materialized in global growth above potential for several years.

This leverage manifested itself in many areas: in the household sector, as households increasingly biased their portfolio allocation toward housing, an area where leverage is typically high and pervasive; in the banking

53

sector via the originate-to-distribute model, as banks were using it mostly as a risk-management tool and not just for liquidity management, and thus, by apparently reducing the level of risk, allowed for increases in leverage; and in the extension of structured credit from corporate bond markets to mortgage markets, an extension that was not straightforward due to the different risk nature of mortgage markets and the lack of history on complete housing-price cycles, thus generating an increase in the implicit leverage of many of these instruments. This was facilitated by the excess demand for AAA assets as a result of the policy of accumulation of excess reserves in many emerging markets. It was therefore a crisis founded on excessive leverage.

Having defined the crisis, we can now proceed to the narrative of the crisis. It can be summarized in one sentence: there were three shocks, each of which changed the paradigm that economic agents had been using for decades. The first was a shock to a key macroeconomic hypothesis, namely that home-price inflation cannot be negative. This hypothesis was embedded in economic and forecasting models, in risk-management systems, in rating agencies' models, basically everywhere. The failure of this hypothesis led to a complete rethinking of our economic outlook.

The second was a shock to a key financial-market product, namely securitization. As Gorton (2008) clearly explains, securitized products transitioned from being informationally insensitive to informationally sensitive. Given how widespread securitization was, this could be compared to a situation where, for example, every banknote in our wallets becomes suspect of being a counterfeit. Citizens would react by first charging a higher price to hold cash and second finding alternative ways of performing transactions. That is exactly what happened with securitization. All of a sudden, every securitized asset became suspect, its value collapsed, and transactions vanished.

The third was a shock to the key liquidity assumption that repurchase agreements, money, and commercial paper markets would continue to function. Suddenly, the rollover of short-term funding could no longer be taken for granted, no matter the cost. It is similar to suddenly realizing that there is no water flowing from the tap. Faced with this event, citizens would run to hoard large amounts of bottled water, and its price would skyrocket. That is exactly what happened: the price of (financial) liquidity increased massively, and economic agents massively increased their precautionary demand for cash.

Each of the shocks by itself may have been harmful but not systemic; however, the combination of all three landed the global economy and markets in the domain of Knightian uncertainty, not knowing which economic model could forecast the outlook, which financial model could price assets, and which financing strategy could fund portfolios. Suddenly, we no longer knew how the world operated. This is the best way to explain the global confidence shock that hit the economy post-Lehman and that yielded the sharp decline in international trade and the synchronized recession since the third quarter of 2008. Companies around the world decided to put their current projects on hold and prepared for the worst-case scenario, canceling orders, laying off workers, hoarding cash, and shutting down capacity.

To these three shocks, the economic authorities reacted with three main policy actions. House-price deflation was a macro shock; thus, the authorities reacted with macro policies, both fiscal and monetary. The securitization shock was an information shock; thus, the authorities reacted with policies to address the information problem, mostly guarantees and central bank funding for those assets. Finally, the liquidity shock led to the collapse of financial intermediation; thus, central banks became the banks of the global financial system by extending the size and term of funding, widening acceptable collateral, and making markets in key assets.

The Knightian uncertainty mostly affected markets' views about the solvency of the global banking sector, thus requiring the implementation of banking-sector rescue packages. However, policymakers were reluctant to admit they faced a full-blown banking crisis and adopted inadequate policies. The length of the turbulence and the successive failures of the initial rescue packages led to the final paradigm change: the belief that policymakers could indeed save the day. To a large extent, the Great Moderation was due to feedback effect of the markets' belief that policymakers would successfully stabilize financial crises—that was the essence of the Greenspan put, which led to lower volatility and higher leverage. As this paradigm was called into question, economic agents started to consider all the worst-case scenarios. No wonder stock markets had retreated in March 2009 to the level of 1995.

It is probably too early to draw definitive lessons from the genesis and management of the crisis, so we will explore four issues where recent experience may have run counter to conventional wisdom. The first issue relates to the economic policy framework. Central banks have had an understood mandate of achieving price stability. This includes the evolution of employment, growth, and prices, but it does not include risk aversion. This crisis has shown that policymakers should move beyond the real economy into the financial economy and embrace the overall stabilization of risk. This implies, on the one hand, stabilizing growth and inflation and, on the other hand, stabilizing risk attitudes within some ranges.

This policy of "risk targeting" is critical to reducing the procyclicality of leverage. The dynamics of value at risk imply that the size of the balance sheet is a direct function of the volatility of asset prices. In a world where policymakers are so predictable that volatility becomes low, value at risk implies balance sheets can be larger for a given level of capital. In other words, policy predictability facilitates higher leverage.[2] So is there an optimal amount of risk in the economy, and how is that related to the optimal amount of transparency that policies, especially monetary policies, can have?

The second issue relates to liquidity management. It has become commonplace to blame financial-sector participants for their overreliance on wholesale markets and their lack of emergency liquidity planning. But one could turn that argument upside down and argue that global policymakers have been fostering the opening up of capital accounts and the development of global and integrated financial markets but have failed to adapt the liquidity facilities at the same pace. Until 2007, central banks were providing liquidity at very short-term maturities, on a narrow set of counterparties and against a narrow set of eligible collateral, and in domestic currency. Clearly, the framework for liquidity provision did not match the reality of global markets. In this regard, the development of foreign exchange swaps at central banks, for example, is a major advance in the global financial system that should be maintained. If that means central banks will be taking more risk, then maybe they should charge for that risk in advance. But they should not refrain from taking the risk as a matter of principle, because otherwise the infrastructure of the financial system will not match the potential needs of the system.

The third issue relates to the management of monetary policy at the zero bound. It is interesting that there are six central banks at the zero bound with six different policy strategies. The Federal Reserve began credit easing via purchases of mortgage-backed securities before reaching zero rates. The Bank of England first hit zero rates and then engaged in purchases of government bonds. The European Central Bank never cut rates to zero but adopted a full allotment provision of liquidity that pushed market rates to the effective zero bound. Sweden's Riksbank cut rates to zero and introduced negative rates on deposits. The Bank of Canada hit zero rates and adopted a time commitment, and the Swiss National Bank cut rates to zero and proceeded to do foreign-exchange intervention. This diversity suggests that the optimal strategy to follow at the zero bound may not be as obvious as it appeared in theory. Furthermore, central banks have hit the zero bound twice in a decade and, given the difficulties and costs associated with monetary policies at the zero bound, it is no longer clear that 2 percent inflation is the right definition of price stability.

In addition, experience shows that leaning against the wind does not work. The recent crisis developed a powerful negative bubble, and monetary policy was powerless against it, having to be complemented by fiscal policy actions and targeted actions in specific sectors particularly affected by the bubble. There is no reason why this approach to the bubble cannot be symmetric; thus, when a positive bubble is developing, actions beyond monetary policy—including tax changes or targeted supervisory or regulatory actions—should be used. A broad and proactive macroprudential policy can provide a buffer to the financial sector that helps cushion the potentially negative effect of a burst bubble, and it may be a superior policy to trying to address overheating asset prices with interest rates.

A lesson from this crisis is the importance of horizontal assessments of the financial sector; in other words, complement bank-by-bank examinations with horizontal examinations of banks' balance sheets by type of product. This is a critical exercise to understand where the crowded positions in the banking sector are and might have allowed a better understanding of the large credit-default-swap volume that was sitting in banks' balance sheets. As far as macroprudential instruments are concerned, dynamic provisioning is probably the best option. It is rules based and defined ex ante, eliminating the many problems associated with discretion and having to define turns in the business cycle—as would be the case with, for example, cyclically adjusted capital ratios or contingent capital.

The fourth and final point is how to deal with future banking crises. The International Monetary Fund has a wide range of publications that provide guidance on how to approach a banking crisis. It is fairly simple: close down the bad/small banks, recapitalize the good/too-big-to-fail banks, and remove the bad assets from the balance sheets. But the recent experience shows that unless there is strong external pressure—an International Monetary Fund package, a currency crisis, or both—the political economy makes it difficult to implement the optimal policy.[3] The political equilibrium requires that some casualties happen before there is an agreement to implement the right policies—which, by including bailouts and use of fiscal resources, are politically costly. Thus the debate regarding a future systemic authority should include whether this authority should internalize this unavoidable delay and, from the very beginning, implement the optimal policy regardless of the distinction of solvency and liquidity, and thus regardless of moral-hazard issues. This would argue for a prefunded investor of last resort and charging ex ante for this insurance.

References

Gorton, Gary. 2008. "The Panic of 2007." In *Maintaining Stability in a Changing Financial System: A Symposium Sponsored by the Federal Reserve Bank of Kansas City.*

Swagel, Phillip. 2009. "The Financial Crisis: An Inside View." *Brookings Papers on Economic Activity*, Spring.

Ubide, Angel. 2008. "Anatomy of a Modern Credit Crisis." *Financial Stability Review*, May.

Notes

1. See Ubide (2008) for a detailed discussion of the causes and evolution of the crisis.

2. See Ubide (2008) for a discussion of the dynamics of value at risk and its relationship to the procyclicality of leverage.

3. See Swagel (2009) for a good discussion of the political economy difficulties that arise in a systemic crisis.

4

Contagion, Culture, and Shadow Banks: Why Some Countries Had Crises and Others Did Not

Greg Ip

October 2009

Determining why some buildings collapse during an earthquake and others do not helps us prepare for future earthquakes. So it is with financial crises. The world has experienced an economic earthquake, yet countries responded differently. Therein lie important lessons as we build a new financial system to replace the old.

As the accompanying table 4-1 demonstrates, the United States and the United Kingdom show the classic symptoms of a crisis economy laid out by Carmen M. Reinhart and Kenneth S. Rogoff in their empirical work (Reinhart and Rogoff 2009) and separately by Ms. Reinhart and Vincent R. Reinhart (2008). They had large, growing current account deficits financed with enormous inflows of foreign savings. Those savings were recycled through their domestic financial systems into the property market. The resulting property bubbles collapsed, triggering banking crises and deep recessions.

However, other countries do not conform to this pattern. Canada, Australia, and Spain had larger housing bubbles than the United States. The latter two had large current account deficits. Yet none of the three have experienced a banking crisis (that is, the collapse or bailout of one or more major institutions).[1] Conversely, neither Germany nor Switzerland had a housing bubble; both had current account surpluses. Yet both had banking crises. Finally, Canada, Japan, and Spain all avoided banking crises, yet all ended up in recessions.

TABLE 4-1
NATIONAL CHARACTERISTICS

	Housing Bubble	Current Account	Banking Crisis	Recession
Australia	Yes	Deficit	No	No
Canada	Yes	Balance	No	Yes
Germany	No	Surplus	Yes	Yes
Japan	No	Surplus	No	Yes
Spain	Yes	Deficit	No	Yes
Switzerland	No	Surplus	Yes	Yes
United Kingdom	Yes	Deficit	Yes	Yes
United States	Yes	Deficit	Yes	Yes

The fact that different countries had different experiences should not distract from the merit of a global explanation for why we had the earthquake in the first place. As Vincent Reinhart notes in the introduction, "A domestic focus neglects the important role of the international sector in both fostering initial excesses and propagating the correction. Such channels of propagation are essential in understanding how the initiating downturn in the US housing market, while large relative to economic activity, produced a stunning contraction in global financial markets."

The crisis has been popularly laid at the feet of the Federal Reserve, which maintained interest rates at 1 to 2 percent from 2001 to mid-2004. But, as Reinhart demonstrates, even when the Fed began to tighten in the second half of 2004, long-term interest rates barely budged. Indeed, long-term interest rates were remarkably low and stable around the world in this period. This requires a global explanation.

The most popular, and the one with which I agree, is the global saving glut: a new and unexpected surge in excess savings from emerging-market countries, in particular China and the oil exporters, looking for a ready home in rich-country bond markets. But monetary policy may also have played a role. Every major central bank, not just the Fed, kept policy rates low in this period. So did many important emerging-market countries that were chained to US monetary policy via fixed exchange rates—most importantly, China. We need more research into how low global policy rates may have interacted with a surge in global savings to produce low long-term rates.

Those low rates and excess savings led to surging credit growth and housing bubbles worldwide. The collapse of the US bubble sparked the crisis, but the ensuing destruction was magnified by high leverage, excess dependence on short-term financing, and overvalued property present in most countries.

What, then, explains why countries experienced this earthquake differently? That many non-crisis countries fell into recession demonstrates the potency of financial and trade linkages in our globalized economy. Japan's and Germany's structurally weak domestic demand exposed them to a collapse in their export markets. Reinhart notes that the United States exported some of its financial innovations to other countries: German and Swiss banks were laid low by dabbling in US mortgages. But such specific linkages are less important than the broad tendency for financial contagion to jump the species barrier, reflecting a generalized flight from risk across time zones and markets. For example, short-term interbank Libor (London Interbank Offer Rates) rates rose everywhere, even in markets like Australia where no banks failed.

Why did some countries, despite severe economic distress, housing bubbles, or both, avoid banking crises, while others did not? The answer lies in the differing structures of their financial systems, including the policy environment.

Unlike Reinhart, I do not assign much blame for the severity of our crisis to the Community Reinvestment Act (CRA) and the government-sponsored enterprises (GSEs) Fannie Mae and Freddie Mac. It is hard to understand why CRA, which was passed in 1977 and broadened in 1993, should suddenly have such a profound impact in the mid-2000s. CRA applied only to banks, yet subprime mortgage origination was dominated by what we used to call nonbanks, until the Pacific Investment Management Company coined the much sexier term "shadow banks" (McCulley 2009). These were principally state-regulated mortgage brokers and finance companies like New Century, the second-largest subprime lender in 2006, which securitized their loans for purchase by private investors and, sometimes, banks. Moreover, a majority of subprime loans did not go to low-income families, the target of CRA; they went to middle- and even upper-income households who often lived in expensive markets like California. A Federal Reserve analysis found that just 6 percent of high-priced loans were made by CRA-covered banks to low-income borrowers or borrowers in their CRA assessment areas (Canner and Bhutta 2008). Banks' loans to low-income borrowers, including CRA loans, have had high delinquencies, but loans made by shadow banks have generally fared worse. One study of a large bank-affiliated mortgage company found that loans it acquired from mortgage brokers were of lower quality and defaulted at higher rates than loans it originated itself (Jiang, Nelson, and Vytlacil 2009). This is not surprising. Banks had stronger incentives than shadow banks to monitor the quality of their underwriting, both because they were more likely to keep the loans on their books and because federal supervision was generally stricter than state supervision.

The GSEs bear a bit more culpability; in 2004, the Bush administration pressed them to increase lending to low-income households, and their purchases of subprime mortgages then rose. But they probably would have anyway. Both GSEs, by the early 2000s, confronted saturation in their main, prime markets. As far back as 2002, Wall Street analysts cited subprime markets as an important source of earnings growth (*Origination News* 2002). From that point on, the GSEs began to increase their presence in both subprime and Alt-A markets.

At the margin, CRA and GSE policy may have encouraged the financial industry to make more risky loans, but this misses the point. In the environment of the 2000s, no such encouragement was needed: the subprime market was growing, and it was immensely profitable. Naturally, lenders were happy to portray such lucrative lending as serving the greater good. In 2003, Angelo Mozilo of Countrywide Financial endorsed President George W. Bush's call to raise minority homeownership rates. Homeownership is "our mission," Mozilo said (Mozilo 2003). Was he motivated more by altruism or profit? A reasonable person would suspect the latter.

Countrywide's enthusiasm for subprime mortgages was shared by countless firms with little or no federal mandate to fulfill, such as CIT Group, which filed for bankruptcy in the fall of 2009, and the investment banks, which significantly expanded their subprime activity when their own capital requirements were loosened in 2004 (Naudauld and Sherlund 2009).

If public policy is to blame, it is for our national obsession with homeownership, irrespective of the economic merits. That is why neither Republicans nor Democrats were sympathetic to policies that would curb subprime activity. Senator Phil Gramm (R-TX), explaining why he opposed a federal antipredatory lending law in 2000, declared, "In the name of predatory lending, we could end up denying people with moderate income and limited credit ratings the opportunity to borrow money" (*Inner City Press* 2000). For the same reason, in 2003 Representative Barney Frank (D-MA) said, "I do not want the same kind of focus on safety and soundness [with GSEs] that we have [toward banks]. I want to roll the dice a little bit more in this situation towards subsidized housing" (US House of Representatives 2003).

These factors are useful for understanding why other countries had housing bubbles but not banking crises. Financial innovation per se is not the reason. After the United States, Australia and Canada have among the most-developed financial systems and deepest asset-backed securities markets (IMF 2006). But there is little subprime activity in them. Australia's "nonconforming" loans, their closest equivalent to subprime loans, accounted for just 1 percent of outstanding loans in 2007, compared to subprime's 13 percent share in the United States, and the US loans generally had higher loan-to-value ratios (Debelle 2008).

More conservative regulation and capital standards almost certainly played a part in the greater resilience of banks in Australia, Canada, and Spain, but such standards must be seen in their local context. Spain experienced one of the modern era's worst bank crises from 1977 to 1982 (Reinhart and Rogoff 2009, 160). In Canada in the early 1990s, numerous trust companies—the equivalent of thrifts—failed or were forced to merge with banks because of real estate and corporate loan losses. Such events shape banking culture in ways not easily explained by laws and capital ratios. As *The Economist* observed of Canada's banks, "It is hard to find pre-crisis equivalents in America of the decision by Toronto-Dominion (TD) to exit its structured products business in 2005, or the 20-30 percent band that RBC [Royal Bank of Canada] imposes on the share of earnings that its capital-markets business can contribute" (2009). Both Canada and Spain began to relax those standards as the last decade's boom rolled on. Fortunately, the bust arrived before they completely caved in.

Still, the main distinction between the United States and these non-crisis countries lies not in how they regulated their banks, but in the importance of banks in the first place. In the United States, banks intermediate only about one-tenth of nonfinancial credit, one of the lowest shares in the Organisation for Economic Co-operation and Development (IMF 2006, 108). The shadow banking system and capital markets do the rest. In part, this reflects historical anomalies: barriers on interstate banking forced banks to accept unhealthy geographic concentrations until securitization helped diffuse those risks. The shadow banking system was also a natural outgrowth of Americans' entrepreneurial culture, and it became a useful laboratory for new types of home, car, mobile home, and consumer loans to borrowers that banks (often because of regulatory restraints) would not touch.

But because of their relatively thin capitalization, their dependence on wholesale funding and securitization markets, and their opacity (in part due to less regulation), shadow banks made the US financial system more vulnerable to a liquidity and solvency crisis. Commercial banks aggravated this vulnerability in their efforts to level the playing field, either by shifting assets to off-balance-sheet vehicles that did not tie up capital, or by acquiring shadow banks, as HSBC did in 2003 with its purchase of Household International, then one of the largest subprime lenders.

Though often forgotten, the subprime crisis did not start out as a banking crisis. It began, arguably, with the announcement of large losses by HSBC Finance (the renamed Household) in early 2007. That was followed by a rash of bankruptcies by nonbank lenders like New Century in 2007, then Bear Stearns's collapse in March 2008, then the GSEs a few months later. Only then did the large commercial banks succumb. (An exception to this rule is thrifts, a type of bank, which had much higher concentrations of exotic mortgages and weaker oversight than other commercial banks.)

This analysis has lessons for current financial system reforms. Our current focus on bank regulation reminds me of the man who looks for his keys under a streetlamp because that is where the light is best, not because that is where he lost them. Banks are more visible, but shadow banking was, and remains, a more important source of risk.

For now, the shadow-system is doing a fine job of shrinking itself. HSBC has come full circle, announcing this year it was winding down HSBC Finance. The two remaining stand-alone investment banks are now bank-holding companies. The GSEs are wards of the Treasury. Yet raising banks' regulatory burdens and capital requirements, as we seem intent on doing, will eventually restore the incentive for risky activity to migrate back to the shadows. While new, or proposed, federal legislation will impose more uniform regulatory and licensing requirements on state-regulated companies, it remains to be seen if the states have the resources and will to enforce them. In 2007, California's Department of Corporations had twenty-five examiners to oversee more than 4,800 state-licensed lenders, including many of the country's largest subprime companies. By comparison, that year forty-six federal bank examiners were assigned exclusively to San Francisco-based Wells Fargo & Co.

And while these proposals seek to spread federal oversight over systemically important nonbanks, it is doubtful regulators will know who those are until it is too late. In fall 1998, the Federal Reserve had only the vaguest notion of who Long Term Capital Management was, much less that some banks it regulated had large exposures to it. Over the long term, our economy prospers because of risk taking and innovation. By their nature, those things flourish where the regulatory burden is lowest: in the shadows. Why would the coming decades be different?

References

Canner, Glenn, and Neil Bhutta. 2008. "Staff Analysis of the Relationship between the CRA and the Subprime Crisis." Mimeograph, Federal Reserve, November 21.

Debelle, Guy. 2008. "A Comparison of the US and Australian Housing Markets." Reserve Bank of Australia. May 16. http://www.rba.gov.au/speeches/2008/sp-ag-160508.html.

IMF (International Monetary Fund). 2006. *World Economic Outlook: Financial Systems and Economic Cycles.* Washington, DC: IMF, September.

Inner City Press Community Reinvestment Reporter. 2000. "July 17-September 25, 2000 (Archive #4 of 2000)." September 25. http://www.innercitypress.org/crrep400.html.

Ip, Greg, and Damian Paletta. 2007. "Lending Oversight: Regulators Scrutinized in Mortgage Meltdown—States, Federal Agencies Clashed on Subprimes as Market Ballooned." *Wall Street Journal,* March 22.

Jiang, Wei, Ashlyn Aiko Nelson, and Edward Vytlacil. 2009. "Liar's Loan? Effects of Origination Channel and Information Falsification on Mortgage Delinquency." Mimeograph. September. http://www.columbia.edu/~wj2006/liars_loan.pdf.

McCulley, Paul. 2009. "The Shadow Banking System and Hyman Minsky's Economic Journey." In *Insights into the Global Financial Crisis*. Charlottesville, VA: CFA Institute, May.

Mozilo, Angelo. 2003. "The American Dream of Homeownership: From Cliché to Mission." Joint Center for Housing Studies, Harvard University, February 4. http://www.jchs.harvard.edu/publications/homeownership/M03-1_mozilo.pdf.

Nadauld, Taylor D., and Shane M. Sherlund. 2009. "The Role of the Securitization Process in the Expansion of Subprime Credit." Federal Reserve Working Paper 2009-28. April. http://www.federalreserve.gov/pubs/feds/2009/200928/200928pap.pdf.

Origination News. 2002. "Market Share Gain Expected for Fannie and Freddie," June 28.

Reinhart, Carmen M., and Kenneth S. Rogoff. 2009. *This Time Is Different: Eight Centuries of Financial Folly*. Princeton, NJ: Princeton University Press.

Reinhart, Carmen M., and Vincent R. Reinhart. 2008. "Capital Flow Bonanzas: An Encompassing View of the Past and Present." National Bureau of Economic Research Working Paper 14321. September. http://www.nber.org/papers/w14321.

The Economist. 2009. "Don't Blame Canada." May 14. http://www.economist.com/specialreports/PrinterFriendly.cfm?story_id=13604591.

US House of Representatives Committee on Financial Services. 2003. "Hearing on H.R. 2575, The Secondary Mortgage Market Enterprises Regulatory Improvement Act." 108th Congress, Washington, DC, September 25. http://commdocs.house.gov/committees/bank/hba92628.000/hba92628_0f.htm.

Note

1. This was true at the time of the October 9, 2009 event. Since then, Spain has had a banking crisis, including the bailout of at least one major institution.

PART II

Financial Experts Respond

5

The Federal Reserve after the Crisis

Frederic S. Mishkin

October 2009

From 2007 to 2009, the financial system in the United States has experienced a disruption that led to unprecedented actions by central banks throughout the world, particularly the Federal Reserve. The events during the recent financial crisis and the Federal Reserve's reactions raise several questions: What should be the regulatory role of the Federal Reserve System, and how should it change? What impact might the actions of the Federal Reserve have on its independence, and what actions should the Federal Reserve pursue in the coming years to preserve it? And how should research at the Federal Reserve (and the economics profession at large) change in the aftermath of the crisis?

The Future Regulatory Role of the Federal Reserve

To examine the future regulatory role of the Federal Reserve, we should first examine why a systemic regulator is needed and why the Federal Reserve is the natural choice for that regulator. We will then turn to what such a regulator should and should not do.[1]

Why We Need a Systemic Regulator. The current framework for prudential regulation and supervision of the US financial system rests on the principle that regulation should ensure the soundness of individual institutions against the risk of loss on their assets. Focusing on individual

69

institutions, however, has obscured the growing importance of the shadow banking system, in which increases in securitization have taken over a substantial amount of lending that was previously done by traditional banks.

There is another respect in which the focus on individual institutions has been problematic. Of course, it is a truism that ensuring the soundness of each institution improves the soundness of the system as a whole. However, it is possible, indeed often likely, that attempts by individual institutions to remain solvent in a crisis can undermine the stability of the system as a whole. If one financial institution lending to a second institution decided to be prudent by cutting lending, this prudent course of action may cause a sharp withdrawal of funding from the second institution (see Morris and Shin 2009). This is precisely the sort of run that happened to Bear Stearns and Lehman Brothers, which ended up crippling both firms. In addition, a focus on individual institution's risks can make boom-bust cycles that lead to severe financial crises, as occurred during the recent episode. In the name of modern, price-sensitive risk-management practices, banks with short-term incentives load up on exposures when measured risks are low, only to shed them as fast as they can when risks materialize, irrespective of the consequences to the rest of the system. The recoiling from risk by one institution generates greater materialized risk for others. It is this spillover to the wider economy that creates the largest social costs. Clearly there is a pressing need to rethink prudential regulation and supervision to focus on systemic risk and to have a regulator with a systemwide perspective.

The Federal Reserve Is the Natural Choice to Be the Systemic Regulator. The US Treasury has proposed that the Federal Reserve act as the systemic prudential regulator and supervisor of the financial system (Geithner 2009). This proposal has met great resistance in Congress. However, there are four strong arguments for having the Federal Reserve be the systemic regulator.

First, the Federal Reserve has daily trading relationships with market participants as part of its core function of implementing monetary policy. As such, it is best placed to monitor market events and to flag looming problems in the financial system. No other institution in the United States has comparable insight and access to the broad flows in the financial system.

Second, the Federal Reserve is the lender of last resort for the financial system, as was amply demonstrated during the crisis. Its balance sheet can be used as a tool in meeting systemic financial crises, and as the lender of last resort, it can provide emergency funding. Too often during the recent crisis, the Federal Reserve was drafted at the last minute to provide funding to an institution in crisis when the central bank had no first-hand knowledge of the institution. Neither Bear Stearns nor American International Group (AIG) was supervised by the Federal Reserve. No amount of information sharing is a substitute for the first-hand information gathered in direct, on-site examinations. There is a strong argument that those in line to put up money to save an institution should supervise that institution.

Third, the Federal Reserve's mandate to preserve macroeconomic stability is consistent with the role of ensuring the stability of the financial system. Macroeconomic policy and macroprudential policy are tailor-made for each other.

Fourth, the Federal Reserve is an independent agency. Successful systemic regulation requires a long-run focus. However, politicians often focus on the short run to get elected. Insulating the systemic regulator from day-to-day interference by politicians is thus an important element to its success. The respect and independence that central banks have make them natural candidates to be systemic regulators.

There are three arguments, however, against the Federal Reserve taking on the role of systemic regulator. First, the clear focus on achieving output and price stability could become blurred once the Fed also takes into account financial-stability objectives. Second, there are legitimate concerns about the Federal Reserve overreaching itself in the resolution stage of a crisis when it greatly extends its balance sheet to lend to private institutions. Third, there are dangers of increased politicization of the Federal Reserve's actions due to its role in the resolution stage of a crisis.

Some safeguards can mitigate the dangers described above. For example, some central banks have used long-run inflation targets to keep the price-stability goal firmly in view, and if the Fed became the systemic regulator, this feature of inflation targeting would be especially valuable.[2] In the resolution stage of crises, a clear demarcation of roles might be able to minimize political pressures on the Fed. Only the fiscal authority (Treasury and the Federal Deposit Insurance Corporation, with approval from

Congress) can authorize the use of public funds. The Federal Reserve as the systemic regulator could assist the fiscal authorities, but they should ultimately be responsible for any resolution effort. If the systemic regulator has performed its prevention role effectively, the need to enter the resolution stage of a crisis will hopefully be very rare.

On balance, the four arguments in favor of having the Fed as a systemic regulator outweigh the arguments against. At a minimum, the four arguments suggest that the Fed should have substantial involvement in systemic regulation. However, concerns in Congress about the Fed becoming too powerful and complaints about its past actions, both as regulator and as a provider of liquidity to the financial system during the crisis, have led some critics of the Fed and politicians to suggest that a committee, with participation from regulatory agencies besides the Fed, be handed the responsibility for conducting systemic regulation and supervision. The problem with this proposal is that no single agency will be ultimately responsible for systemic regulation, so a likely outcome is that systemic regulation will not be sufficiently strong. Furthermore, there is always political infighting that occurs between regulatory agencies, and having these agencies jointly conduct systemic regulation would slow down decision making and could lead to watered-down systemic regulation. Because systemic regulation is so important, leaving it to a committee could have negative consequences for the health of the financial system.

What Should the Fed as a Systemic Regulator Do? The primary role of the systemic regulator should be to prevent financial crises. But how should it do this?

First, as a systemic regulator, the Federal Reserve should gather, analyze, and report systemic information that would point out potential emerging dangers to the financial system. This would require reporting from a broad range of financial institutions, with standardized position values and risk exposures. The Fed should then analyze and disseminate this information by preparing periodic reports to Congress, just as it currently does for monetary policy. Other central banks have begun publishing *Financial Stability Reports,* so there is already precedent for this kind of reporting.

Second, the Federal Reserve should design and implement financial regulations with a systemic focus. Capital requirements for regulated financial institutions should be higher for institutions that pose more systemic risk to the financial system, both because they can do more damage and because they are more likely to be viewed as too big to fail, and thus are more likely to receive government bailouts when they get into trouble. The greater likelihood of bailouts for these institutions means that they are likely to be subject to less market discipline and will therefore have greater incentives to take excessive risks. For example, large banks holding illiquid assets and relying heavily on short-term debt to finance their activities should be required to hold more capital than smaller banks with liquid assets and less-volatile financing arrangements. The Federal Reserve should design and administer these capital requirements and should negotiate with regulatory authorities in other countries to ensure that capital requirements are comparable internationally, a process that it has already been engaged in with the Basel Accords.

What Should the Federal Reserve Not Do? The Fed has been handed tasks by Congress that are not central to its mission and that could interfere with its role as a systemic regulator. The Fed not only conducts monetary policy and is a bank regulator, but it is also a consumer regulator under the Truth in Lending Act. This causes two problems. One is that protecting consumers involves setting and then enforcing the appropriate rules under a transparent legal framework. Such work is primarily done by lawyers specializing in rule making and enforcement. The orientation of an effective systemic regulator must be different from that of a rule-enforcing consumer-protection agency or from that of a business regulator. A regulator charged with enforcing rules and managing systemic risk may eventually devote too much of its attention to rule enforcement.

Another problem is that consumer regulation is highly charged politically. Because consumer regulation affects so many constituents, politicians sometimes put tremendous pressure on regulators to protect consumers without worrying about unintended consequences. Political pressure from politicians who are unhappy with the Fed's role as a consumer regulator may interfere with its independence and thus its ability to conduct monetary policy and perform systemic regulation.

The above arguments indicate that the Federal Reserve should get out of consumer regulation because it can interfere with good monetary policymaking. Taking on the role of systemic regulator makes it even more imperative that the Fed get out of consumer regulation, because engaging in consumer regulation exposes the Fed to even greater political risk.

Dangers to Federal Reserve Independence

Economic theory provides strong support for the independence of central banks. Both successful systemic regulation and successful monetary policy require a focus on the long run. Subjecting central banks to short-run political pressure makes it more likely that the monetary policy authorities will try to exploit the short-run tradeoff between unemployment and inflation by pursuing excessively expansionary monetary policy to lower unemployment—with a long-run outcome of higher inflation, higher interest rates, and yet no better performance on the unemployment rate. Indeed, empirical evidence supports central bank independence, with less independent central banks having worse performance than more independent ones.[3] This is one of the reasons that governments throughout the world have granted increased independence to their central banks. Unfortunately, the Federal Reserve's independence has come under increasing attack in the aftermath of the recent financial crisis, and this poses serious dangers for the economy.

Why the Fed's Independence Is in Danger. A striking feature of the recent crisis was the huge expansion in the Federal Reserve balance sheet as a result of its large liquidity injections into the credit markets to try to get them lending again. Over the course of the crisis, the Fed broadened its provision of liquidity to the financial system well outside of its traditional lending to depository institutions, leading Paul Volcker, a former chair of the Federal Reserve, to describe the Fed's actions as going to the "very edge of its lawful and implied powers" (Volcker 2008).

Many of the liquidity injections had a fiscal element because they put risk on the Fed's balance sheet that could impose substantial losses to the taxpayer in the future. Thus, Volcker's comment should not be seen as a criticism of the Fed: it is a statement of fact. The Fed's actions were extraordinary and involved taking unprecedented risk onto its balance sheet.

There are several reasons for these actions. First, one lesson from past financial crises is that the faster action is taken to backstop the financial system, the less severe and shorter the crisis is (Mishkin 1991). Because central banks can generate liquidity out of thin air, they can provide it far faster than any government entity. For example, in the recent crisis the Federal Reserve intervened almost on a moment's notice in the Bear Stearns episode, both in effect purchasing Bear Stearns's toxic assets and setting up a liquidity facility, the Primary Dealer Credit Facility, to contain contagion to other investment banks.

Second, the Fed in effect took fiscal actions because political constraints hampered the government's ability to deal with the crisis. Unfortunately, the crisis hit during a lame-duck presidency that was weakened by low popularity ratings. Extraordinarily, after the Lehman bankruptcy and the AIG bailout, when the Bush administration proposed an allocation of $700 billion for the Troubled Asset Relief Program (TARP), it was opposed most strenuously by the president's own political party. Although the four-day delay in passing TARP after it was initially voted down may seem short, it had important economic consequences. It signaled that the US government was unlikely to act rapidly with policies to deal with the crisis.

The situation did not improve when the Obama administration came into power. Public anger over government bailouts has become more intense over time, particularly when large sums of taxpayer money are used without imposing sufficient restrictions to limit payments to shareholders and other stakeholders, such as the management of the troubled firms. A striking example is the anger over the $165 million in bonuses paid out to AIG employees, some of whom can be blamed for the speculative behavior that helped make this crisis so damaging. As a result, Congress was unwilling to allocate additional funds to clean up the financial system, and the Obama administration was unwilling to ask. By March 2009, the nervousness in the markets reached an extremely high level, and credit spreads went through the roof. Aggressive Fed intervention was then necessary to stabilize the financial markets.

The Bernanke Fed had to deal with the following tradeoff. On the one hand, if it did not step in to stabilize the financial system, there was a serious probability that the economy could experience a depression. On the other hand, the Fed's actions moved it in the direction of conducting fiscal policy by taking so much private risk onto its balance sheet. This possible overreaching of the Fed's mandate has two consequences. First, the Fed's actions to stabilize the financial system increase moral hazard. If the Fed is backstopping the system, market participants will expect the Fed to do so in the future, resulting in less market discipline to restrain risk taking. Second, going to the legal limits of its authority to engage in these fiscal actions was politically risky and would likely lead to attacks on the independence of the Fed.

These attacks are exactly what transpired. The Senate passed a nonbinding resolution that not only asked the Fed to publish the nature and amounts of collateral it accepted in its various lending programs, along with information that could be used to figure out the individual borrowers it lent to, but also included an evaluation of the appropriate number and associated costs of the Federal Reserve Banks. This evaluation is a not-too-subtle attack on Federal Reserve independence because it would weaken a key part of the Federal Reserve System: the Federal Reserve Banks.

A more recent attack was launched by Representative Ron Paul (R-TX), who sponsored a bill to subject the Federal Reserve's monetary policy actions to the Government Accountability Office audit. Rep. Paul is a well-known foe of the Federal Reserve who has called for its abolishment. It is not remarkable that he sponsored such a bill. What is extraordinary is that 250 of his fellow representatives cosponsored the bill.

Fed chairman Ben Bernanke had to weigh both elements of this trade-off—a possible depression if the Fed did not act, or a loss of independence if it did—and came down squarely on taking actions to prevent a depression. He went out on a limb because he saw the danger of inaction to be much greater than the danger of the loss of Fed independence.

What Should the Fed Do to Protect Its Independence? Given the Fed's actions to prop up the financial system and recent criticism of its regulatory activity—particularly over financial products for consumers, some of whom found that they were given loans they could not repay—the Federal Reserve is in a difficult position. Preserving its independence is therefore a high priority. One way to do this is to exit the large balance sheet positions that leave the Fed politically exposed.

Particularly dangerous in this regard is the Fed's holdings of mortgage-backed securities (MBS). Housing finance is probably the most politicized part of capital markets in the United States. Politicians of all stripes see homeownership as highly desirable, and government intervention in housing finance to encourage homeownership has been particularly massive. This includes tax deductibility of mortgage interest payments and government guarantees of residential mortgages. It also helps explain why Congress provided such strong support for Fannie Mae and Freddie Mac's expansion of their housing-loan portfolio, even though they were taking excessive risks that would likely cost taxpayers a lot of money.

The longer the Federal Reserve is involved in housing finance with its huge holdings of MBS, the greater the likelihood that politicians will want this to become permanent, thus further politicizing the Fed. The Fed has already wound down some of its balance sheet positions, some of which are dying a natural death as the credit markets improve. However, to stimulate housing demand and help the value of securities based on housing loans recover—an important element in the recovery of the financial system as a whole—the Fed bought over a trillion dollars of MBS purchases. Although this made sense given the weakness of the housing market and the overall economy, it presents the Fed with the following dilemma: how is it going to exit the MBS market?

Exiting the MBS market will not be easy, because selling off this portfolio will lead to higher residential mortgage rates. Not only will this in effect be a tightening of monetary policy, but it will surely lead to intense criticism of the Fed. Think about all the real estate brokers and home builders who will be up in arms and complaining to their congressional representatives. Nonetheless, selling off this portfolio, not too far in the future and certainly before the current chairman ends his term, has to be the highest priority. The timing will be tricky. First, it will be important that these sales not disrupt the market. This argues for them to done over a substantial period of time. Just as the Fed has decided to extend the purchases of MBS over a fairly long period, it will need to sell them over a long period as well, and the Fed will need to announce a plan to do so. Second, an announcement of the sales will cause mortgage rates to rise. The Fed will not want this to happen until financial markets are on a sustained path to recovery. However, the Fed should start the sales as soon as it is safe, in order to reduce the political risk the holdings create. This means that the Fed should not wait until the economy is fully recovered before doing so.

Macroeconomic Research at the Federal Reserve and Elsewhere

A series of articles in the popular press, *The Economist* (2009) and Krugman (2009) in particular, have criticized the economics profession and research at central banks. These articles argue that macroeconomics has completely missed out on understanding the dangers from financial disruptions and how policymakers should deal with them. These articles also imply that macroeconomic research over the last thirty years has lost its relevance.

These articles, in my view as well as that of others, are completely off base (for additional critiques, see Lucas 2009; Cochrane 2009). Macroeconomic research on financial frictions played a particularly prominent role in informing central banks about how they should respond to the financial disruption that began in August 2007. Chairman Bernanke is one of the important contributors to the literature on the role of financial frictions in business-cycle fluctuations (Bernanke 1983; Bernanke and Gertler 1989; Bernanke, Gertler, and Gilchrist 1996), and I, another member of the Board of Governors of the Federal Reserve, also contributed to this literature (Mishkin 1978; Mishkin 1991). When the financial disruption first manifested itself in August 2007, the board staff considered this research in thinking about the evolution of the economy, both by developing and tracking measures of financial stress and by modifying their forecasts by putting large, negative add-factors into their macroeconometric models.

As a result of this analysis, the Federal Reserve took aggressive actions early in the financial crisis to ease monetary policy. Immediately after the shock from the suspended redemption of shares held in some money market funds by BNP Paribas, which caused a substantial widening of credit spreads, the Fed lowered the discount rate by fifty basis points (0.50 percentage points). Then at the Federal Open Market Committee meeting in September 2007, the Fed reversed course and lowered its federal funds target. Importantly, these steps to ease monetary policy and pump liquidity into the financial system were taken when the economy still had positive momentum and when inflation was rising to well above any reasonable target level for the Federal Reserve.

Contrary to the view expressed in the press that macroeconomic research was irrelevant and uninformative during the crisis, it actually led to a more aggressive response to counteract the negative effects from the financial disruption than otherwise would have been the case.

There are, however, serious criticisms that need to be addressed. The problem that central bank researchers and the macroeconomics profession now faces is that, although we have research that indicates the importance of financial crises to business-cycle fluctuations, this research has not been incorporated into general equilibrium models. Neither DSGE (dynamic stochastic general equilibrium) models used at central banks nor older more traditional econometric models such as the FRB/US model—the primary econometric model used for policy analysis and forecasting at the Federal Reserve—have financial frictions built into them as a key factor that can affect economic activity. This is a major failing.

The good news is that the recent crisis is likely to reinvigorate general equilibrium macroeconomic research. Researchers at central banks are now focusing on financial frictions, as are many macroeconomists in academia. The representative-agent framework in many DSGE models is likely to be challenged. However, many of the lessons learned from the more micro-founded modeling that led to DSGE models will be essential features in future general-equilibrium macro models that embed financial frictions. The central role of expectations in these models and the management of expectations in thinking about policy will be at the forefront of these new modeling efforts. Research at central banks and in the macroeconomics profession in general will indeed be very exciting in coming years. Just as the Great Depression of the 1930s and the Great Inflation of the 1970s led to exciting research in macroeconomics, the financial crisis starting in 2007 is likely to do the same. Indeed, we may enter a new golden era of macroeconomics in the coming years.

References

Alesina, Alberto, and Lawrence H. Summers. 1993. "Central Bank Independence and Macroeconomic Performance: Some Comparative Evidence." *Journal of Money, Credit, and Banking* 25: 151-62.

Bernanke, Ben S. 1983. "Nonmonetary Effects of the Financial Crisis in the Great Depression." *American Economic Review* 73: 257-276.

Bernanke, Ben S., and Mark Gertler. 1989. "Agency Costs, Net Worth, and Business Fluctuations." *American Economic Review* 79: 14-31.

Bernanke, Ben S., Mark Gertler, and Simon Gilchrist. 1996. "The Financial Accelerator and the Flight to Quality." *Review of Economics and Statistics* 78: 1-15.

Cochrane, John H. 2009. "How Did Paul Krugman Get It So Wrong?" University of Chicago manuscript (September 16) http://faculty.chicagobooth.edu/john.cochrane/research/papers/krugman_response.htm

French, Kenneth R. et al. 2010. *The Squam Lake Report: Fixing the Financial System* (Princeton, NJ: Princeton University Press).

Geithner, Timothy. 2009. "Treasury Secretary Tim Geithner Written Testimony House Financial Services Committee Hearing." March 26. http://www.treasury.gov/press-center/press-releases/Pages/tg67.aspx

Krugman, Paul. 2009. "How Did Economists Get it So Wrong?" *New York Times Magazine* (September 2) at http://www.nytimes.com/2009/09/06/magazine/06Economic-t.html

Lucas, Robert E., Jr. 2009. "In Defense of the Dismal Science," *The Economist* (August 6) http://www.economist.com/node/14165405

Mishkin, Frederic S. 1978. "The Household Balance-Sheet and the Great Depression." *Journal of Economic History* 38 (December): 918-937.

———. 1991. "Asymmetric Information and Financial Crises: A Historical Perspective." In *Financial Markets and Financial Crises*, edited by R. Glenn Hubbard, 69-108. Chicago, IL: University of Chicago Press.

———. 2009. "In Praise of an Explicit Number for Inflation." *Financial Times*. January 11.

Morris, Stephen, and Hyun Song Shin. 2009. "Financial Regulation in a System Context." *Brookings Papers on Economic Activity*, Spring.

The Economist (2009). "The Other-Worldly Philosophers" (July 16) http://www.economist.com/node/14030288

Volcker, Paul. 2008. Speech given at the Economic Club of New York, April 8, 2008, as quoted in Bloomberg, http://www.bloomberg.com/apps/news?pid=newsarchive&sid=aPDZWKWhz21c

Notes

The views expressed here are the author's own and are not necessarily those of Columbia University or the National Bureau of Economic Research. Disclosure of the author's outside compensated activities can be found at www0.gsb.columbia.edu/faculty/fmishkin/.

1. This section draws on chapter 2 of French et al. (2010) that I was involved in writing.

2. There are many other reasons why moving to an inflation target would be beneficial, as I have argued elsewhere (Mishkin 2009).

3. Alesina and Summers (1993) is the classic reference.

6

Determinants of the Size of Fiscal Multipliers in Open Economies

Ethan Ilzetzki, Enrique G. Mendoza, and Carlos A. Végh

November 2009

As fiscal stimulus packages were hastily put together around the world in 2009, one could not have been blamed for thinking that there must be some broad agreement in the profession regarding the size of the fiscal multipliers. Far from it. In a January 2009 *Wall Street Journal* op-ed, Robert Barro argued that peacetime fiscal multipliers are essentially zero. At the other extreme, Christina Romer, chair of President Barack Obama's Council of Economic Advisers, used multipliers as high as 1.6 in estimating the job gains that would be generated by the $787 billion stimulus package approved by Congress in February 2009. The difference between Romer's and Barro's views of the world amounts to a staggering 3.7 million jobs.

If anything, the effects of fiscal policy are even more uncertain in developing and emerging markets than in the United States. Data are more scarce and often of dubious quality. A history of fiscal profligacy and spotty debt repayments calls into question the sustainability of any fiscal expansion. How does this financial fragility affect the size of fiscal multipliers? Does the exchange regime matter? What about the degree of openness? These are all critical policy questions that remain largely unanswered.

A big hurdle in obtaining precise estimates of fiscal multipliers has been data availability. Most studies have relied on annual data, which makes it difficult to obtain precise estimates. To address this shortcoming, we have put together a novel quarterly dataset for forty-four countries (twenty high-income and twenty-four developing).[1] The coverage, which varies across countries, spans from 1960:1 to 2007:4. We have gone to great lengths to ensure that only data originally collected on a quarterly basis are included (as opposed to interpolated based on annual data). Using this unique database, we have estimated fiscal multipliers for different groups of countries in our sample.[2]

The main results of our study—presented in greater detail below—can be summarized as follows:

- In developing countries, the response of output to increases in government spending is smaller on impact and considerably less persistent than in high-income countries. This is partially due to the fact that output's response to a government spending shock becomes negative in the medium run (after approximately three years).

- The degree of exchange-rate flexibility is a critical determinant of the size of fiscal multipliers. Economies operating under predetermined exchange-rate regimes have long-run multipliers of around 1.5, but economies with flexible exchange-rate regimes have essentially zero multipliers.

- The degree of openness to trade (measured as exports plus imports as a proportion of gross domestic product [GDP]) is another critical determinant.[3] Relatively closed economies have long-run multipliers of around 1.6, but relatively open economies have very small or zero multipliers.

- In highly indebted countries, the output response to increases in government spending is short lived and much less persistent than in countries with a low debt-to-GDP ratio. In the medium run, the response of output to government spending shocks is actually negative in highly indebted countries.

- The multipliers for the United States in the post-1980 period are rather small (in the range of 0.3–0.4), both in the short and long run. However, multipliers for government investment are large (around 2).

- To set the stage for the subsequent discussion of our results, we will first briefly review the current state of knowledge on the subject of fiscal multipliers.

What Do We Know about Fiscal Multipliers, and How Do We Know It?

In addition to the existing debate on the size of fiscal multipliers, there is substantial disagreement in the profession regarding how to identify fiscal shocks. This identification problem essentially arises because there are two possible directions of causation: (1) government spending could affect output, or (2) output could affect government spending (through, say, automatic stabilizers and implicit or explicit policy rules). How can we make sure that we are isolating the first channel and not the second?

There have been two main approaches to addressing this identification problem: (1) the Structural Vector Autoregression (SVAR) approach, first used for the study of fiscal policy by Blanchard and Perotti (2002), and (2) the "natural experiment" of large military buildups first suggested by Barro (1981) and further developed by Ramey and Shapiro (1998) to account for expectations. Rather than using military buildups per se to identify fiscal shocks, Ramey and Shapiro use news of impending military buildups (through reporting in *Business Week*) as the shock variable.

The basic assumption behind the SVAR approach is that fiscal policy requires some time (which is assumed to be longer than one-quarter) to respond to news about the state of the economy. After using a VAR to eliminate predictable responses of the two variables to one another, it is assumed that any remaining correlation between the unpredicted components of government spending and output is due to the impact of government spending on output. The possible objection is that these identified shocks, while unpredicted by the econometrician, may have been known to private agents.

The natural experiment approach relies on the fact that it is very unlikely that military buildups may be caused by the state of the business cycle, and thus are truly exogenous fiscal shocks. The objections to this approach are: (1) military buildups occur during or in advance of wars, which might have a macroeconomic impact of their own, and (2) two military buildups (World War II and the Korean War) dwarf all other military spending, so this instrument essentially consists of two observations (Hall 2009).

The existing range of estimates in the SVAR literature varies considerably, particularly across the few Organisation for Economic Co-operation and Development (OECD) countries that have been studied so far. Specifically, Blanchard and Perotti (2002) find a multiplier of close to 1 in the United States for government consumption. Perotti (2004, 2007), however, shows that estimates vary greatly across (five OECD) countries and across time, with a range of −2.3 to 3.7. Other estimates for the United States— using slight variations of the standard SVAR identifying assumption—yield values of 0.65 on impact but −1 in the long run (Mountford and Uhlig 2008) and larger than one (Fatas and Mihov 2001).

In the "natural experiment" literature, Ramey (2011) extended and refined the Ramey and Shapiro (1998) study using richer narrative data on news of military buildups and finds a multiplier of close to 1. She also shows that SVAR shocks are predicted by professional forecasts and Granger-caused military buildups, a critique of the SVAR approach. Using a similar approach, Barro and Redlick (2011) find multipliers on government consumption in the 0.6 to 0.7 range. Fisher and Peters (2010), however, address possible anticipation effects by resorting to stock prices of military suppliers as an instrument for military spending and find a multiplier of 1.5.

In sum, not only do estimates vary greatly, but they essentially come from four to five OECD countries. Other than this—and to the best of our knowledge—no high-frequency study has been conducted on fiscal policy in a larger set of countries, and particularly of countries outside the OECD. Thus, our contribution is novel in this sense. This not only gives us a sample size that is larger by an order of magnitude than most existing studies (close to 2,500 observations, compared to approximately 200 in those of the United States) and therefore more accurate estimates, but also allows us to split the sample in various ways that shed light on how the impact of government spending differs depending on each country's specific macroeconomic policies and conditions.

High-Income versus Developing Countries

As a first cut at the data, we divided the sample into high-income and developing countries. Figure 6-1 shows the impulse response of GDP to a 1 percent shock to government consumption at time 0. While the impact response is higher in high-income countries (0.05 percent) than in developing countries (0.01 percent), the most striking difference is how much less

FIGURE 6-1

OUTPUT RESPONSE TO A 1 PERCENT SHOCK TO GOVERNMENT CONSUMPTION

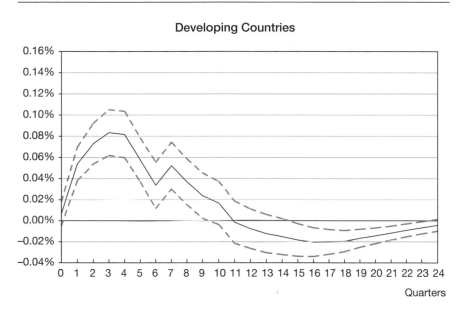

Developing Countries

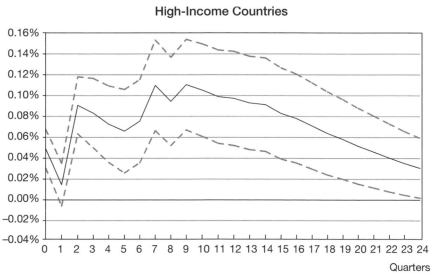

High-Income Countries

SOURCE: Authors' calculations.
NOTE: Dotted lines indicate the one-standard-deviation significance band.

persistent the output response is for developing countries. Indeed, while the output response for high-income countries remains significantly positive for the twenty-four quarters covered in the plot, it becomes zero (statistically speaking) after about only ten quarters for developing countries, before turning *negative* after approximately three years.

Based on the impulse response depicted in figure 6-1, we can compute the corresponding fiscal multipliers. The impact multiplier for high-income countries is 0.24.[4] In other words, an additional dollar in government spending will deliver only twenty-four cents of additional output in the quarter in which it is implemented. For developing countries, the impact multiplier is close to zero.

Focusing on the impact multiplier, however, may be misleading because fiscal stimulus packages can only be implemented over time, and there may be lags in the economy's response. To account for these factors, figure 6-2 shows the *cumulative* multipliers for both high-income and developing countries, defined as the cumulative change in GDP divided by the cumulative change in government consumption (as a percentage of GDP). For example, a value of 0.5 in quarter three would indicate that, after three quarters, the cumulative increase in output, in dollar terms, is half the size of the cumulative increase in government consumption. The plots also include the value of the long-run cumulative multiplier.[5]

We can see that the cumulative multiplier for high-income countries rises from an initial value of 0.24 (the impact effect) to a long-run value of 1.04. Hence, even after the full impact of a fiscal expansion is accounted for, output has essentially risen by the same amount as government consumption. On the contrary, the cumulative long-run multiplier for developing countries is just 0.79.[6] In other words, in the long run, an additional dollar of government consumption crowds out some other component of GDP (investment, consumption, or net exports) by twenty-one cents.

Predetermined versus Flexible Exchange-Rate Regimes

As a second cut at the data, we divided our sample of forty-four countries into those with predetermined exchange rates and those with more flexible exchange-rate regimes.[7] The cumulative impulse responses, shown in figure 6-3, suggest that the exchange-rate regime matters a great deal.

FIGURE 6-2

CUMULATIVE MULTIPLIER IN RESPONSE TO A SHOCK TO GOVERNMENT CONSUMPTION

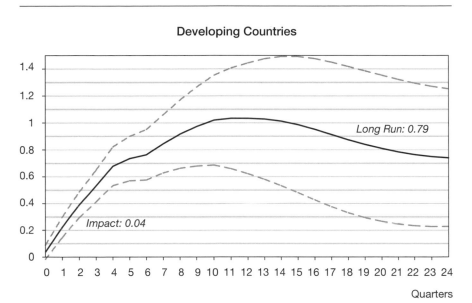

Developing Countries

Long Run: 0.79

Impact: 0.04

Quarters

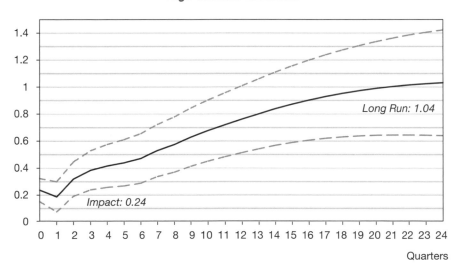

High-Income Countries

Long Run: 1.04

Impact: 0.24

Quarters

SOURCE: Authors' calculations.

FIGURE 6-3

CUMULATIVE MULTIPLIER:
PREDETERMINED AND FLEXIBLE EXCHANGE-RATE REGIMES

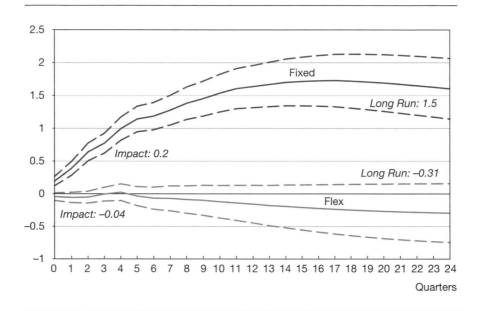

SOURCE: Authors' calculations.

Under predetermined exchange rates, the impact multiplier is 0.2 (and significantly different from zero) and rises all the way to 1.5 in the long run. Under flexible exchange-rate regimes, however, the multiplier is indistinguishable from zero both on impact and in the long run.

These results are, in principle, consistent with the Mundell-Fleming model, one of the workhorses of modern open-economy macroeconomics, which predicts that fiscal policy is more effective in stimulating output under predetermined exchange rates than under flexible exchange rates. In this model, the initial effect of a fiscal expansion is to increase output and raise interest rates, which tends to appreciate the domestic currency. Under predetermined exchange rates, the monetary authority must expand the money supply to prevent this appreciation. Such monetary policy accommodation provides an additional boost to output. Under flexible exchange rates, however, the monetary authority keeps a lid on the money supply,

FIGURE 6-4

CUMULATIVE MULTIPLIER: OPEN AND CLOSED ECONOMIES

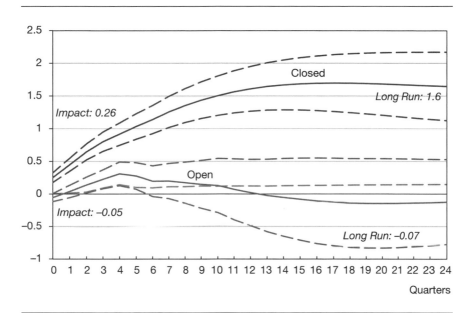

SOURCE: Authors' calculations.

which cuts short any further output expansion. The model, however, finds it difficult to explain *no* change in output under flexible exchange rates, as our findings suggest.

Open versus Closed Economies

As a third cut at the data, we divided our sample of forty-four countries into open and closed economies. For our purposes, we defined as open a country whose foreign trade (imports plus exports) exceeds 60 percent of GDP. If foreign trade is less than 60 percent of GDP, we defined the country as closed. (Minor variations of this definition did not significantly affect our results.) Using this criterion, twenty-nine countries are classified as open and the remaining fifteen are classified as closed. The cumulative responses, shown in figure 6-4, indicate that the degree of openness is a critical determinant of the size of the fiscal multiplier. For the closed economies, the impact response is 0.26 and reaches 1.6 in the long run. For the open economies, both the impact and the long-run response are not significantly different from zero.

These results are, in principle, consistent with a standard Keynesian view of the world in which the multiplier is lower in a more open economy, as a larger fraction of the fiscal expansion is diverted to the rest of the world through higher imports.

Financial Fragility

Our final cut at the data was to divide developing countries into highly indebted countries (countries with an external debt-to-GDP ratio above 50 percent; eleven countries in total) and countries with low debt (less than 50 percent; fourteen countries in total). Figure 6-5 shows the impulse response of GDP to a 1 percent shock to government consumption at time 0. While the short-term response is larger for highly indebted countries than for low-debt countries, the most striking feature is how short-lived the GDP response is in the case of highly indebted countries. In fact, the GDP response becomes zero (statistically speaking) after just four quarters and significantly negative after ten quarters.

This finding is consistent with the idea that, in highly indebted countries, the sustainability of any rise in government spending will be quickly called into question by market participants. The resulting increase in financing costs will not only make it more difficult to keep up the fiscal expansion but also dampen the output effects of current government spending.

What about the United States?

Given the ongoing debate in the United States regarding the effectiveness of Obama's fiscal stimulus package—captured by the debate between Barro and Romer in the introductory paragraph—it is certainly relevant to inquire about the size of fiscal multipliers for the United States. This continues to be relevant these days as politicians in the United States and around the world debate the relative merits of fiscal stimulus and fiscal austerity.

The top panel in figure 6-6 shows the cumulative multiplier for the United States for our whole sample (from 1960 to 2007). The impact

FIGURE 6-5

OUTPUT RESPONSE TO A 1 PERCENT SHOCK TO GOVERNMENT CONSUMPTION

Debt/GDP < 50%

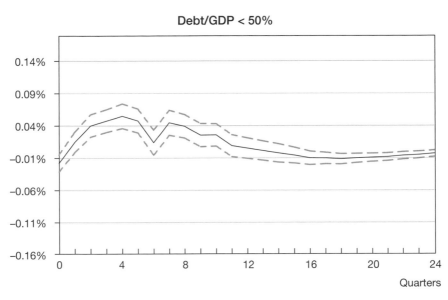

Debt/GDP > 50%

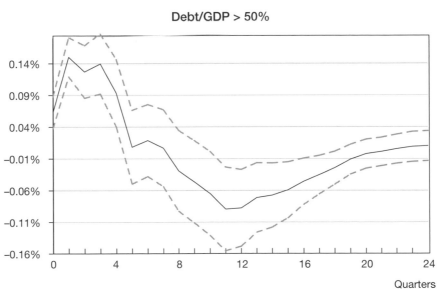

SOURCE: Authors' calculations.

multiplier is 0.64, and the long-run cumulative multiplier is 1.19. While these estimates are certainly closer to Romer's than to Barro's, they mask some important structural changes over the sample period. To see this, consider the bottom panel in figure 6-6, which breaks the sample into pre-1980 and post-1980.

The difference between the two subsamples is quite striking.[8] The pre-1980 multipliers are considerably larger than the post-1980 multipliers. The post-1980 multipliers are just 0.32 on impact and 0.4 in the long run.[9] This is certainly a far cry from the impact multiplier (1.05) and long-run multiplier (1.55) used in the Romer report.[10]

While the reasons for the dramatic change in fiscal multipliers for the United States from the pre- to the post-1980 period deserve a more careful analysis, we conjecture that, in line with our previous findings, two factors have played an important role. First, while for most of the pre-1980 period the United States operated under the Bretton Woods system whereby the value of the dollar was officially fixed to gold, during the post-1980 period the United States has operated under a fairly flexible exchange-rate regime. Higher exchange-rate flexibility has allowed a greater emphasis on controlling inflation since the Volcker disinflation in the early 1980s to the more recent de facto inflation targeting pursued by the Federal Reserve. The focus on price stability has left little scope for monetary accommodation during fiscal expansions. Second, the United States has become a much more open economy, as evidenced by the fact that its ratio of exports plus imports (as a proportion of GDP) has increased from 12 percent in the earlier subsample to 22 percent in the later.

In practice, a sizable component of Obama's package consists of government investment, as opposed to government consumption. Figure 6-7 shows the cumulative multiplier for government investment in the United States for the post-1980 period. The multipliers are 2.31 on impact and 1.83 in the long run. While the precision of the estimates falls as the horizon lengthens, we can see that the cumulative multiplier is significantly different from zero for around fourteen quarters. In sharp contrast—and as already noted—the post-1980 multipliers for government consumption are not significantly different from zero at *any* horizon. Differentiating between government consumption and investment is thus a critical consideration.

FIGURE 6-6
CUMULATIVE MULTIPLIER: UNITED STATES

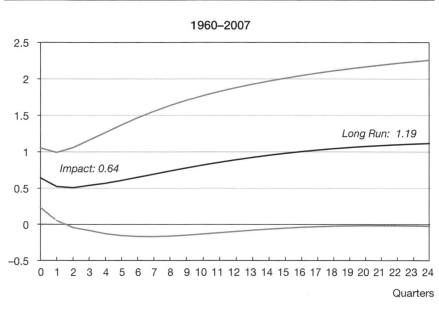

1960–2007

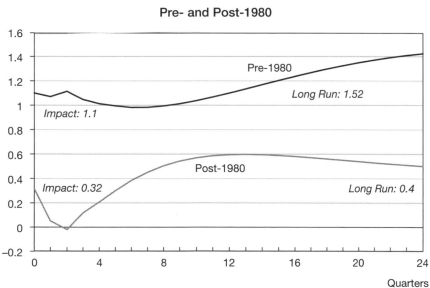

Pre- and Post-1980

SOURCE: Authors' calculations.

FIGURE 6-7

CUMULATIVE MULTIPLIER ON GOVERNMENT INVESTMENT:
UNITED STATES (1980–2007)

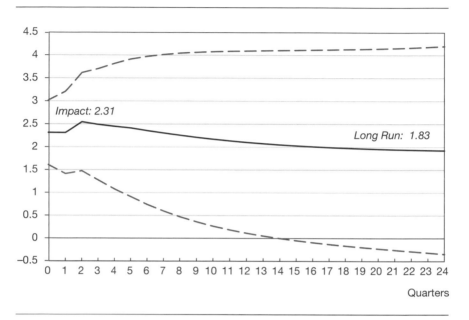

SOURCE: Authors' calculations.

Policy Implications

All in all, our findings suggest that drawing sweeping generalizations on
the size of the fiscal multipliers is probably an exercise in futility. Some of
our most robust results point to the fact that the size of the fiscal multipliers critically depends on key characteristics of the economy (closed versus
open, predetermined versus flexible exchange-rate regimes, high versus low
debt) or on the type of aggregate being considered (government consumption versus government investment).

In particular, we have found that, in economies open to trade and operating under flexible exchange rates, a fiscal expansion leads to no significant output gains. Further, any gains will be, at best, short-lived in highly
indebted countries. Since, over the last decades, many emerging countries
have become more open to trade and moved toward greater exchange-rate

flexibility (typically in the context of inflation-targeting regimes), our results suggest that seeking the holy grail of fiscal stimulus is likely to be counterproductive, with little benefit in terms of output and potential long-run costs due to larger stocks of public debt.

Emerging countries—particularly large economies with some degree of "fear of floating"—would be well served if they stopped pursuing procyclical fiscal policies. Indeed, emerging countries have typically increased government consumption in good times and reduced it in bad times, thus amplifying the underlying business cycle—what Kaminsky, Reinhart, and Végh (2004) have dubbed the "when it rains, it pours" phenomenon. The inability to save in good times greatly increases the probability that bad times will turn into a full-fledged fiscal crisis. Given this less-than-stellar record in fiscal policy, even an acyclical fiscal policy—whereby government consumption and tax rates do not respond to the business cycle—would represent a major improvement in macroeconomic policy. While occasional rain may be unavoidable for emerging countries, significant downpours would be relegated to the past.

Finally, for the case of the United States, we have found that the fiscal multipliers for the post-1980 period are rather small and, in fact, not significantly different from zero. Hence, based on our analysis, we expect increases in government spending in the United States to have little effect on growth and jobs. The multipliers on government investment, however, are much larger and significantly different from zero for more than three years. The *composition* of any stimulus package is thus bound to be a key variable when it comes to assessing the growth effects of any stimulus package.

References

Barro, Robert J. 1981. "Output Effects of Government Purchases." *Journal of Political Economy* 89: 1086-1121.

———. 2009. "Government Spending Is No Free Lunch." *Wall Street Journal*, January 22.

Barro, Robert, and Charles J. Redlick. 2011. "Macroeconomic Effects from Government Purchases and Taxes." *Quarterly Journal of Economics*, 126:1.

Blanchard, Olivier, and Roberto Perotti. 2002. "An Empirical Characterization of the Dynamic Effects of Changes in Government Spending." *Quarterly Journal of Economics*, 1329–1368.

Fatás, Antonio, and Ilian Mihov. 2001. "The Effects of Fiscal Policy on Consumption and Employment: Theory and Evidence." CEPR Discussion Paper 2760.

Fisher, Jonas D. M., and Ryan Peters. 2010. "Using Stock Returns to Identify Government Spending Shocks." *Economic Journal,* 120:544.

Hall, Robert. 2009. "By How Much Does GDP Rise If the Government Buys More Output?" *Brookings Papers on Economic Activity,* September.

Ilzetzki, Ethan, Carmen Reinhart, and Kenneth Rogoff. 2009. "Exchange Rate Arrangements Entering the 21st Century: Which Anchor Will Hold?" Mimeograph, University of Maryland and Harvard University.

Ilzetzki, Ethan, Enrique G. Mendoza, and Carlos A. Végh. 2012. "How Big (Small?) Are Fiscal Multipliers?" Forthcoming in the *Journal of Monetary Economics.*

Kaminsky, Graciela, Carmen Reinhart, and Carlos Végh. 2004. "When It Rains, It Pours: Procyclical Capital Flows and Macroeconomic Policies." *NBER Macroeconomics Annual.*

Mountford, Andrew, and Harald Uhlig. 2008. "What Are the Effects of Fiscal Policy Shocks?" NBER Working Paper 14551.

Perotti, Roberto. 2004. "Estimating the Effects of Fiscal Policy in OECD Countries." Mimeograph, Bocconi University.

————. 2007. "In Search of the Transmission Mechanism of Fiscal Policy." NBER Working Paper 13143.

Ramey, Valerie A. 2011. "Identifying Government Spending Shocks: It's All in the Timing," *Quarterly Journal of Economics,* 126:1.

Ramey, Valerie A., and Matthew D. Shapiro. 1998. "Costly Capital Reallocation and the Effects of Government Spending." *Carnegie-Rochester Conference Series on Public Policy,* 48, no. 1: 145-194.

Romer, Christina, and Jared Bernstein. 2009. "The Job Impact of the American Recovery and Reinvestment Plan." Council of Economic Advisers, January.

Notes

This chapter summarizes the main findings in Ilzetzki et al. (forthcoming), where a more detailed analysis can be found.

1. Most of our developing countries would be viewed as emerging countries, so we will use both terms interchangeably.

2. Technically, we have estimated a vector autoregression model using the cyclical components (i.e., deviations from quadratic trends; results are similar using deviations from linear trends) of GDP and government consumption and then computed the impulse response of GDP to a change in government consumption. Our identifying assumption, following Blanchard and Perotti (2002), is that discretionary government consumption can only respond to output with a one quarter lag.

3. We should note that this definition of openness, based on actual trade activity, would not necessarily coincide with a definition based on the degree to which a

country allows for free international trade (that is, the size of tariff and nontariff barriers). A case in point is the United States, a relatively closed economy based on actual trade activity, but highly open based on actual restrictions to trade.

4. To arrive at the impact multiplier for, say, high-income countries, we simply divide the impact effect in figure 6-1 (0.05 percent) by the ratio of government consumption to GDP (0.21), which gives us 0.24.

5. The long-run multiplier is the value that the cumulative multiplier takes, once the responses of both GDP and government consumption have died down. Notice that this may not coincide with the value of the cumulative multiplier after twenty-four quarters, when our plots end.

6. In more recent work (Ilzetzki et al., forthcoming), we were able to incorporate important updates to the dataset and found that while qualitatively the results are similar, quantitatively, the multipliers for developing countries are significantly smaller than for industrial countries.

7. We followed the updated Reinhart-Rogoff classification in Ilzetzki, Reinhart, and Rogoff (2009).

8. Our findings for the United States are consistent with those reported by Perotti (2004).

9. To avoid cluttering, we have omitted the significance bands in the right panel of figure 6-6. They would show that the pre-1980 multipliers are significantly different from zero only for the first five quarters and that the post-1980 estimates are never significant. We should caution, however, that the sample for the United States is about eight times smaller than that for high-income countries as a whole.

10. We should also caution that the multipliers reported by Romer and Bernstein (2009) refer to a *permanent* increase in government spending, rather than a temporary (though persistent) increase as is typical of VARs.

7

Exit Strategies and the Federal Reserve

Ricardo Reis

January 2010

Quite a few remarkable changes took place in the United States economy in the final years of the 2000s. House prices fell more and faster than in the last one hundred years, seemingly powerful banks closed their doors forever, and the economy went into the largest recession since the Great Depression. These and other changes were amply dissected by the media. But one other change went largely unnoticed by the general public: the Federal Reserve System and the conduct of US monetary policy changed more in the last two years of the 2000s than perhaps any other time since the system's inception in 1913.

The Fed, as it is commonly called, has for most of its history limited its actions to buying and selling government bonds from a select group of banks in exchange for money that it puts into circulation. It has also lent money to a few banks directly, for short periods of time and against sound collateral, and has bought and sold some gold and foreign currencies. In 2008-09, the Fed extended its reach in ways that few had imagined before. It made loans to a myriad of institutions, started buying securities directly like a regular investor, and found itself supporting failed companies like Bear Sterns and American International Group (AIG). While discussions about the Fed had before only referred to the state of the economy and the odds of a recession, since then there have been questions about the state of the Fed's balance sheet and the odds it could suffer heavy losses in its investments. While the Fed still sets interest rates, the news about the Fed is now more often about discussions in Congress about its powers, or the successes and failures of its latest credit programs.

For the most part, these changes were not planned well in advance. They did not follow long debates, with arguments discussed in numerous conferences and opposing views put forward in the public arena. This is perhaps why most people have not realized that something has changed. Rather, the Fed has been forced to react and adapt to the unusual circumstances of a financial crisis that few had anticipated.

The goal of this chapter is to look forward to how the Fed should proceed in the future. It starts with a brief review of the main changes before turning to three main questions. First, what are the dangers of the current situation? There are both economic and political concerns, namely the potential tradeoff between controlling inflation and economic stability, and the role of the Fed within the US government. Second, can the Fed get back to its traditional role? A catchphrase for the discussion of the future of monetary policy has been "exit strategies," referring to the ways in which the Fed could return to its customary state of affairs. This chapter discusses the viability of these strategies. Finally, should the Fed revert back to this customary state? Some of these changes may have been desirable even without a crisis. Now that the Fed has them, it may be a good idea to keep them.

Extraordinary Times

At the most basic level, a central bank is the sole entity that can put currency into circulation and set minimum requirements for the amount of reserves other banks must hold. While there are many definitions of money, one that is both simple to understand and that the Fed controls well is the sum of currency in circulation and the reserves that banks hold, mostly in deposits at the Fed. This is called the monetary base.

In December 2007, the monetary base was $836 billion, approximately 6 percent of annual gross domestic product (GDP) that year. By December 2009, the monetary base had grown to $2,026 billion, about 14 percent of that year's GDP. This 142 percent increase in the monetary base is especially shocking, given that the average two-year increase in the monetary base between 1959 and 2007 was 13 percent, and the highest-ever increase was 24 percent. This change was also not short lived: in April of 2012, the monetary base was $2,640 billion. There is more money in the US economy than ever before, and it has grown many times faster than it ever had.

There is another measure of money, M1, which equals currency in circulation plus checking deposits. This matches more closely what people in their everyday lives think of as money. If banks were required to keep as reserves all of their deposits, sometimes called full-reserve banking, then M1 and the monetary base would be the same. Instead, banks can use the deposits to make loans, keeping only a fraction as reserves. In this world of fractional reserve banking, bank loans are deposited by other people, leading to M1 exceeding the monetary base. The ratio between the two is called the money multiplier.

Looking at the data on M1, it was equal to $1,395 billion in December 2007. Two years later, it had risen to $1,724 billion. While impressive, this increase is considerably smaller than the increase in the monetary base. This contrast uncovers the main reason for the increase in the base: a rise in the reserves held by banks. The money multiplier has fallen, or in other words, banks have been making fewer loans, preferring to keep their customers' deposits stored inside the Fed's vault. These two events, the rapid increase in the monetary base and the large decline in the money multiplier, have not occurred in this magnitude at any time in the last fifty years.

Most people identify the Fed not with money but with interest rates. Since the early 1990s, the Fed has been publicly announcing targets for the federal funds rate, the interest rate in the federal funds market, where a select group of banks lends money to each other overnight. How can the Fed set a market price like an interest rate? By using its ability to issue money to buy and sell government bonds from some of these banks in exchange for crediting the reserve accounts of these banks at the Fed, it seamlessly controls the demand for money in the federal funds market, thereby effectively controlling the interest rate. These are called open-market operations, and because the buying and selling of government bonds takes place every day, the Fed only interacts with a small group of nineteen banks. These banks are sufficiently large and credible, so the Fed need not worry about having these transactions honored.

Looking at the target for the federal funds rate, available since December 1982, interest rates are now lower than they had ever been. From December 2008 onward, the Fed has been announcing that it is targeting a value for the federal funds rate between zero and 0.25 percent, and, as of April of 2012, the Fed continues to keep the rate at this low value. Zero is not just the lowest the interest rate has been, it is also approximately the lowest it can be. If the interest rate is negative, banks would prefer to hold on to the reserves rather than lend them to other banks, and people in turn would prefer to hold cash in their pockets rather than pay a bank to hold them. The interest rate can be slightly negative, as keeping money in one's pocket may be inconvenient and there is a chance it can be stolen or lost, but there is still a lower bound on interest rates, which is plausibly quite close to zero.

There has been another significant change in the Fed's policy regarding interest rates. Starting in October 2008, the Fed began paying interest on the reserves that banks deposit at the Fed. The expense that this involves has been small, given that the interest rate set by the Fed has been only 0.25 percent since December 2008. But paying interest on reserves is an entirely new tool at the disposal of the Federal Reserve, one that it never had before.

Of all these changes, perhaps the most remarkable is the composition of the Fed's assets. Since the end of the Bretton Woods system, the Fed has traditionally held mostly US Treasuries that it can use in its open-market operations. The only other relevant assets are small amounts of gold and foreign currency. As a result, the Fed's balance sheet has traditionally taken less than one page, changing little from year to year. The only relevant default risk in this balance sheet has been the remote chance that the US Treasury defaults on its debt.

Since 2007, the balance sheet has expanded to many pages, including multiple assets with different default risks and a myriad of financial firms on which the Fed now has credits. Some of these changes have come through a menu of different liquidity programs that the Fed introduced in 2007 and 2008, dealing with new financial institutions in forms never tried before. The most conservative is the Term Auction Facility (TAF), through which the Fed now lends to a wider set of banking institutions providing credit for twenty-eight or eighty-four days, with terms determined by auction. Because this credit is given against high-quality collateral, the risk default is low. Its desirability stems from the fact that banks have access to funding for longer than just overnight. Slightly more distant from the Fed's usual actions is the Term Structure Lending Facility (TSLF) and the Primary Dealer Credit Facility, through which the Fed also gives credit overnight and at twenty-eight days against collateral, but to primary dealers of securities. The third set of programs extended credit to even more financial firms, many of which had never engaged in transactions with the Fed. This was composed of the Asset-Backed Commercial Paper Money Market Mutual Fund Liquidity Facility and the Money Market Investor Funding Facility, where credit was provided to money market funds. Finally, the Fed entered a series of swap agreements with foreign central banks, through which it exchanged dollars for their currency, with a promise to receive the dollars back in a short period of time.

The next set of liquidity programs was more out of line with the tradition of the Fed. Through the Term Asset-Backed Securities Loan Facility, the Fed lent widely, accepting as collateral any asset-backed security as long as it was rated AAA and backed by student, auto, credit card, and small business loans. For commercial standards, the default risk is small, but, by the Fed's standards of traditionally accepting nothing but Treasury securities for collateral, the risk is quite high. The final liquidity facility is the Commercial Paper Funding Facility, through which the Fed was willing to lend against commercial bonds issued by companies that had trouble selling them to private agents in the markets. De facto, the Fed started providing credit to some US nonfinancial firms.

Most of these programs were terminated by 2010, or are very close to having zero balances by 2012. Their legacy for the future is the precedent that, if there is another financial crisis, the arsenal of tools at the Fed's disposal is now much wider.

Beyond these loans, the Fed also started buying assets directly. The first innovation was the purchase of mortgage-backed securities (MBS), in an attempt to provide some demand in a market that has been deeply affected by the financial crisis and prevent a rise in mortgage rates. The second innovation was the creation of a series of corporations (Maiden Lane LLCs) that purchased assets from Bear Sterns and AIG, as part of the government bailout of these companies. The Fed also made loans to Citigroup and Bank of America, although these have been repaid for the most part.

Finally, since 2009, the Fed bought large amounts of agency debt guaranteed by the United States government, notably debt issued by Fannie Mae and Freddie Mac, as well as longer-term government bonds. By holding these long-term bonds, the Fed's plans for interest rates for the next few years now have a direct impact on the value of the assets the Fed holds.

All of these programs combined means that the Fed's balance sheet is radically different from what it was at the start of 2007, before the financial crisis. The Fed went from dealing with only a few banks, and facing almost no risk in its mostly government assets, to making loans to and buying assets from a myriad of different private agents, with different risks associated both with changes in the price of these assets as well as with possible defaults on the loans. Whereas before the crisis, the large majority of the Fed's assets were short-term government bonds, as of April of 2012, these accounted for less than 5 percent of its assets. By 2012, most liquidity programs and loans have ended, and the bulk of the Fed's assets are mortgage-backed securities, agency debt, and government bonds, all of medium or long maturities.

These three changes—an increase in the amount of liquidity, historically low interest rates, and a whole new set of Fed investments—illustrate that while the Fed's buildings and staff remain largely unchanged, its role in the economy has changed dramatically. Is this dangerous, and if so, in what way? How can the Fed get back to its old mode of operations, or should it keep some of these innovations? These questions will be tackled next.

What Are the Dangers of the Current Situation?

The Federal Reserve's mandate, as determined by law, is "to promote effectively the goals of maximum employment, stable prices and moderate long-term interest rates." Because it is conventionally understood that the third of these goals follows if the first two are achieved, this law is often referred to as the dual mandate. In the current context, this mandate begs the question: what are the dangers of these changes to the Fed's procedures when it comes to inflation and employment in the present and next few years?

The Dangers for Inflation. A powerful strand of economic thought, called monetarism, links inflation to the growth rate of money. Milton Friedman famously said that "inflation is always and everywhere a monetary phenomenon." Looking at the evolution of the monetary base should provide some insights on what will happen to inflation. This is indeed the simple model that undergraduates in macroeconomics still learn. With the monetary base

FIGURE 7-1

YEAR-ON-YEAR INFLATION SINCE JANUARY 2000
FOR PERSONAL CONSUMPTION EXPENDITURES

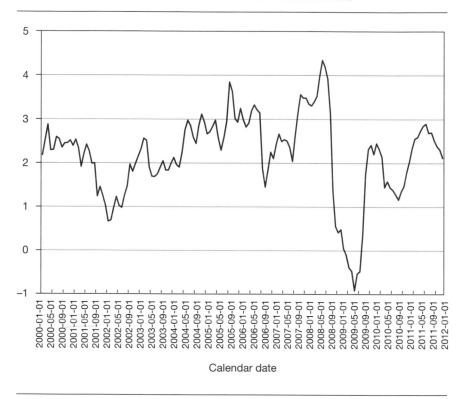

Calendar date

SOURCES: Author's calculations, Federal Reserve Economic Data (FRED), Federal Reserve Bank of Saint Louis, Personal Consumption Expenditures, Chain-Type Price Index (PCEPI).

rising faster than it ever has, a naïve application of monetarism would lead to expecting unprecedentedly high inflation, well into the double digits.

However, figure 7-1 shows year-on-year inflation since January 2000. In this ten-year period, inflation rose slightly until it peaked in 2008 a little above 4 percent; it then fell sharply to the neighborhood of zero in 2009 and has not exceeded 3 percent since. But one might ask, "What about future inflation?" Instead of offering one particular, and surely flawed, prediction of the future, one can look at surveys for what economists think. While only a few surveys of expected inflation more than a few years out exist, one of the most used is the Survey of Professional Forecasters, which provides inflation forecasts for the next five and ten years. According to the numbers released in May 2012 surveying forty-one forecasters, the median forecast is 2.35 percent for 2012 through 2016 and 2.48 percent for 2012 through 2021.[1] In November 2007, just as the crisis was starting, these forecasts were 2.5 percent and 2.4 percent respectively. There is little evidence that inflation is getting out of hand.

This apparent disconnect between theory and reality arises because the aforementioned theory was too naïve and flawed to apply to current times. A more sophisticated application of monetarism suggests that linking the growth rate of the monetary base to inflation relies on two pillars. The first is that the money multiplier is stable. Then, and only then, does an increase in the monetary base track an increase in M1. The second pillar is a stable relationship between interest rates and the amount of money people want to hold, so that there is a link between M1 and the price of goods. Both of these pillars fail when nominal interest rates are zero, as they have been in the United States.

The money multiplier breaks down because at a zero percent interest rate, banks are indifferent between holding new printings of money as excess reserves and lending them out. Whereas with positive interest rates, banks want to hold as few reserves as possible and usually hold only the minimum legal requirements, a zero percent interest rate involves banks holding large reserves. Therefore, an increase in the monetary base does not imply an increase in M1, and the money multiplier falls. While the monetary base has increased at an extraordinary rate, the growth rate of M1 during the recession, while high on average, is not so out of line with what was seen in 1987, 1993, or 2001–2003.

The relationship between interest rates and money demand also breaks down because at a zero interest rate, people are not rushing to exchange any extra money for goods. When someone decides to hold money, the loss is the forgone interest that could have been earned by buying a bond. With a positive nominal, fixed interest rate, an increase in the amount of M1 must come with an increase in prices of similar proportion so the real amount of money held by people is still in line with the interest rate. In other words, if there is more money in the system, but the same number of goods being produced and motivating the desire to hold money, then the price of these goods in dollars must go up. But when the nominal interest rate is zero, people are happy to hold as much money in the bank as there is out there, as long as it is enough for them to engage in their transactions. There is no new demand for goods, and therefore no reason to expect inflation.

If, with a zero nominal interest rate, the monetary base is no longer a reliable signal of the evolution of inflation, then what takes its place? A related theory of what determines inflation that works more reliably at a zero nominal interest rate looks not at money but at nominal interest rates directly. As with the monetarist theory, it is based on two pillars. The first is the Fisher equation, named after the late economist Irving Fisher. It states that the interest rate is equal to inflation plus a real interest rate, which is higher when consumption is growing faster. The second pillar is the premise that the central bank chooses to target the nominal interest rate with an aggressive response to inflation, increasing the federal funds rate by more than one if inflation goes up by 1 percent. Most evidence seems to show that this has been the case for the last twenty-five years in the United States, and this policy has received the name the "Taylor principle," after economist John B. Taylor.

Combining these two premises leads to the conclusion that inflation is determined by a weighted average of current and future interest rates as well as current and future economic growth. If the economy is expected to go into a deep recession, real interest rates are pushed down, which for a given nominal interest rate pushes down inflation. Alternatively, lowering nominal interest rates below what the rate of inflation justifies according to the usual policy choice has the effect of raising inflation.

This theory provides a different interpretation of recent events. A deep recession pushed inflation down to the point where, without intervention by the Fed, US consumers might have seen prices falling. The Fed lowered the federal funds rate as low as it could, all the way down to zero, trying to push inflation up. This has not been enough to offset the effect of the recession on inflation, so the United States has experienced lower-than-usual inflation, in spite of the aggressive monetary expansion.

What about the risk of future inflation? It depends mostly on what happens to interest rates in the future. There are no signs that the Fed will keep interest rates this low for longer than absolutely necessary. As soon as a recovery in the economy gets underway and inflation gives signs of picking

FIGURE 7-2

THE THREE MAIN RECESSIONS OF THE LAST ONE HUNDRED YEARS:
2007–09, 1981–83, AND THE GREAT DEPRESSION

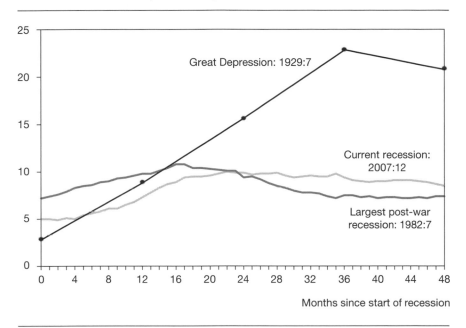

SOURCES: FRED, Federal Reserve Bank of St. Louis; "Unemployment during the Great Depression," *Historical Statistics of the United States*, Millennial Edition, Series ba475, http://hsus.cambridge.org/ HSUSWeb/.

up, raising interest rates would be enough to keep inflation under control. According to this theory, the present situation only brings dangers to inflation insofar as the Fed will be too slow to act in the future. Otherwise, there is no reason to expect an increase in inflation.

The Danger for Employment. The danger for employment is clear: that the United States may slip into a depression as in the 1930s. Thus, it is helpful to start by comparing the 2007-09 recession with the 1981-83 recession, previously the largest recession in the postwar United States, as well as with the first few years of the Great Depression. Figure 7-2 plots the unemployment rate in the United States since December 2007, when the recession officially started, together with the same measure starting in July

1981, as well as unemployment during the start of the Great Depression using circles to represent the available annual data. The figures show the data until four years after the peak of the business cycle, therefore including some of the recovery.

The recession of 2007–09 is clearly visible. Both in level and in the rate of change, unemployment was as bad as, or worse than, anything the country had seen in the postwar period. The recovery and fall in the unemployment rate have also been painfully slow. Still, the United States is far from the catastrophic events of the Great Depression. As exceptionally bad as times are, the last recession did not spiral into a depression.

Whether this was caused by the financial crisis, by events in the real economy, or by a third factor perhaps causing both is not the point of this chapter. The goal is instead to understand what the Federal Reserve can do to stop this increase in unemployment.

Conventional wisdom says that lowering nominal interest rates, or printing money, is the answer. The lower return on savings that this monetary stimulus induces would encourage people to increase the demand for goods today, boosting production and employment. However, the interest rate is already at zero; it cannot go down any further.

The danger is that even a zero nominal interest rate may not be enough. To see why, recall the Fisher equation stating that nominal interest rates equal real interest rates plus expected inflation. Imagine now that the crisis in the US economy is so serious that it would take significantly negative real interest rates to stimulate spending. If inflation expectations are sticky at around 2 percent, as the surveys seem to show, then lowering nominal interest rates to their lower bound of zero will at best generate slightly negative real interest rates. In this case, even though they are already negative, real interest rates are still too high, and thus employment is too low, relative to what may be desirable.

By driving the nominal interest rate to zero, is the Fed already doing all it can to combat unemployment? In theory, no, since raising inflation expectations would lower the real interest rate and stimulate the economy. Since, ultimately, the Fed affects inflation by setting nominal interest rates, the arguments of the previous section suggest that if the Fed were able to credibly commit to keeping nominal interest rates at zero for a prolonged period of time, it should be able to raise inflation expectations.

The Fed's policy announcements have been clear that it will do all it can to prevent inflation from becoming negative, including keeping nominal interest rates at zero for as long as it takes. It therefore seems that, at least according to theory, the Fed is trying to minimize the employment risks as far as it can.

Another way of stating this commitment to lower nominal interest rates for a prolonged period of time is to try to lower long-term nominal interest rates today. The Fed has also moved in this direction by shifting the composition of the Treasury securities it holds from short-term Treasury bills to long-term Treasury bonds. Buying Treasury bonds may raise their price and lower their return, but more importantly it provides a signal of the commitment to keep interest rates low in the future.

The Danger to the Fed's Independence. Whereas the dangers for employment and inflation were related to the novelties in interest-rate and money-supply policies, the danger for the Fed's independence is mostly tied to the new assets on the Fed's balance sheet. It is a less direct but potentially more long-lasting challenge.

The motivation for the several liquidity programs was to promote financial stability. While this is not explicitly an objective of the Fed, there is a presumption (justified by the Great Depression) that financial instability can turn a recession into a depression. The Fed lent to different financial agents and bought assets in different financial markets usually with the goal of keeping those markets operating and ensuring that the financial system as a whole was still reallocating funds from lenders to borrowers.

While almost all of these programs had been terminated by 2012, this venture into unfamiliar territory comes with two great dangers looking forward. By interfering in many domains that were previously under the sole oversight of Congress and the Treasury, the Fed has raised questions regarding its independence relative to these bodies. The Fed is an independent entity, though it is governed by the rules put forth by Congress. Given the goals set by the Federal Reserve Act, it has the autonomy to set monetary policy in whatever way leads to stable inflation and employment, without any direction from the president or interference from Congress. The Fed manages its own budget and is only directly influenced by Congress and the president at the time of the appointment of the governors of the Federal Reserve.

One of the great lessons in the study of central banking in the last twenty years is that independent central banks can achieve both lower inflation and more economic stability. This has been confirmed by several empirical studies and has found support in theories that partly gave a Nobel Prize to Finn Kydland and Edward Prescott. An independent central bank is able to resist pressure from the government to print a little more money either to pay for government debts or to slightly increase employment. Because markets and people realize this, independent central banks are more credible and lead to lower inflation expectations and interest rates, as well as more stable employment.

However, these virtues of central bank independence applied to the old regime, in which the Fed kept its job narrowly constricted to putting money into circulation and buying and selling marginal amounts in the deep Treasury securities market. Once the Fed started intervening in many other markets, this raises legitimate questions as to how these markets were chosen, and within them, why some securities were purchased instead of others. More to the extreme, participating in the bailout of some financial companies like AIG and Bear Stearns, but not others, sometimes in close cooperation with the Treasury, raises the issue of using public money without congressional approval in a stretched interpretation of the Fed's mandate.

A related danger of congressional interference in the conduct of monetary policy is that, by taking on risky assets, the Fed incurs losses. This is particularly worrying for the assets in Maiden Lane associated with Bear Stearns and AIG, as well as for the MBS. In normal times, the risk of any losses in Treasury security holdings is small. Since it collects some seigniorage revenues from issuing money, the Fed usually has more than enough funds to run its operations and is still left with enough funds to remit to the Treasury. But if the Fed suffers a substantial loss, it may find itself without funds to pay its bills. Two potential sources of funds would be to sell some of these assets or to issue reserves. If both of them are incompatible with the employment and inflation goals of the Fed, the only other alternative is to ask for funds from Congress. Once this happens, it is only a small step for Congress to start conditioning how monetary policy is conducted, effectively ending the independence of the Fed.

The chance that the Fed suffers such large losses that it needs to turn to Congress for funds is still remote. Yet, the possibility has already emboldened members of Congress to attack the Federal Reserve Act and remove some of the Fed's independence that has had such beneficial effects over the past few decades.

It is important to emphasize that, given what is known today, there is no reason to doubt that the Fed has done nothing but pursue financial stability and general welfare in the US economy. The Fed has been more transparent than most government agencies, explaining carefully the rationale behind most of its actions, in spite of the confidentiality constraints that come with some of its loans. Moreover, given how quickly events took place in the financial markets, the Fed was often the only agent of the US government that could respond, even if in an ideal, better-designed regulatory system, a branch of government would have stepped in.

The final danger to the Fed's independence is subtler and more remote, but still one to bear in mind. By engaging in financing relations with so many financial institutions, the Fed has become an important agent in many markets, and has opened the door for future interventions. Financial-market participants now have available a strategy that they did not have two years ago: to lobby the Fed to intervene and cover their losses. When the Fed dealt only with banks, and heavily regulated them in exchange for rare interventions, this problem may have been under control. Once the Fed entered into credit transactions with so many other financial firms, the resulting moral hazards cracked the natural barrier preventing them from trying to steer policy in ways that are privately profitable but socially costly.

Can the Federal Reserve Get Back to Its Usual, Precrisis Role?

Regarding interest rates, the answer is a clear yes. Nothing prevents the Fed from raising its target for the federal funds interest rate. Likewise, even though the Fed now has the power to pay interest on reserves, it has full freedom to set the rate of interest at whatever level it chooses, including zero forever. Returning to the precrisis policy regime regarding interest rates would be easy.

Reversing the more than doubling of the monetary base would be a little harder, although it still falls within the normal set of actions used by the Fed. If the federal funds rate rises above the interest rate paid on reserves, banks would again face a cost of holding money on reserves. The money multiplier would go back to normal, and as banks tried to unload their excess reserves, the Fed could stand ready to absorb it by giving them government bonds in return. Standard open-market operations, the bread and butter of the Fed's activities, should naturally take care of lowering the amount of money in circulation.

Turning to the assets of the Fed, the multiple liquidity programs (TAF, TSLF, etc.) consisted of loans with durations of at most three months. By simply letting them expire, the Fed was able to eliminate them almost entirely by 2010. The terms at which these loans were made were quite onerous for the borrowers. Once credit conditions returned to normal, they were glad to let them go.

Reversing the maturity of the Treasury securities it holds would not be difficult. The Fed could simply sell the Treasury bonds it holds and use the proceeds to buy Treasury bills. This could be accomplished in a few weeks. The markets for these securities are sufficiently liquid that, if done in an orderly fashion, this would have a small impact on their operation. It may cause some challenges for the Treasury in managing the desired maturity of outstanding public debt, but there is no reason why they would not be able to deal with these challenges. This change does not even need to affect private holdings of government securities, since if the Treasury does the reserve purchases and sales, the operation becomes just a matter of accounting between these government and semipublic entities.

So far, reversing the changes of the past two years does not seem particularly hard. More complicated is the sale of the $858 billion of MBS held by the Fed.[2] This action was motivated by the contraction in demand for these securities during the financial crisis, perhaps as a result of the fall in prices in the housing market and the deterioration of the finances of households with mortgages due to the economic crisis. The Fed acted to prevent increases in mortgage rates, or even at points in the financial crisis to offset the near absence of MBS financing for new mortgages in the housing market. Unlike the liquidity programs, which have gradually unwound, the holdings of MBS have been stable since 2010, and in May 2012 accounted for about 30 percent of all the assets held by the Fed.

To reduce its MBS holdings, the Fed could just hold them and collect their payments until they mature. However, this could take many years: while the Fed has not revealed the maturity of its portfolio of MBS, if it resembles the maturity of securities outstanding in the market, it is more than just a few years. Moreover, the value of the MBS will fluctuate over time, exposing the Fed to considerable financial risk.

Alternatively, the Fed could gradually sell these securities, as the market for housing recovers and the private demand for MBS reappears. There are two difficulties with this strategy. First, it is unclear that the Fed would be the best "market timer" at selling its positions, so again there is a risk of incurring unexpected losses. Moreover, with the Fed as such a large holder of these securities, it may start paying for speculators to try to time the Fed itself. Many central banks around the world have faced these challenges in the last thirty years in another market, as they tried to reduce their holdings of gold, and have learned from this experience that doing it well requires time and patience.

A second difficulty with selling the portfolio of MBS goes back to the Fed's independence. The Fed's holdings are approximately 10 percent of the outstanding amount in this market—not a small deal, especially as mortgages have a high political visibility and the issuers of these MBS are Fannie Mae, Freddie Mac, and Ginnie Mae, government-sponsored enterprises that have for decades relied on support and implicit guarantees from Washington. The Fed may again come against political pressure in the management of its MBS that diverts its focus from the dual mandate and jeopardizes its independence.

Should the Federal Reserve Get Back to Its Old Ways?

Having discussed how the Fed could undo the many changes since the financial crisis, this section turns to the question of whether it should do so. Starting with the changes in the Fed's assets, there is no compelling reason why the support of AIG and Bear Stearns, the holdings of MBS, or the many short-term liquidity programs should be continued. These actions are justified in response to the financial and credit crisis. Once these crises are gone, however, there is no reason to keep them. Moreover, as was already discussed, these assets come with the danger of capture by financial participants, and they may lead the Fed to lose focus from its dual mandate of maximum employment and price stability. Finally, by intervening directly in some financial markets for a prolonged period of time, the Fed would inevitably be interfering with the incentives in those markets in ways that are not justified by its mandate and would not lead to any clear gain in efficiency. Going back to a boring Fed balance sheet, with Treasury securities as the main item on the asset side, may be best.

There is one exception to this broad conclusion: the TAF. This liquidity program extends the actions of the Fed from the small set of primary dealer banks to potentially many more banking institutions. Instead of only buying and selling Treasury securities from them, the Fed can lend to banks for twenty-eight or eight-four days at terms determined by auction. This is one extra useful tool at the disposal of the Fed in conducting "plain vanilla" monetary policy. Indeed, many central banks, including the European Central Bank, have had similar mechanisms in place for some time. It provides one way for the Fed to inject liquidity quickly into the banking sector and to obtain valuable information from the market price at which the auctions clear.

Turning to interest rates, raising them is less clearly good or bad. On the one hand, as was discussed in the context of the risks for inflation, raising interest rates once the economy starts recovering is crucial to ensure that inflation remains low and under control. On the other hand, as was discussed in the context of the risks for employment, keeping nominal interest rates low for a prolonged period of time may be the more effective way to raise inflation expectations, lower the real interest rate, and stimulate the economy. Pursuing this more expansionary policy requires the Federal Reserve's willingness to accept the risk of higher inflation in exchange for the prospect of less unemployment, a familiar dilemma for monetary policy.

The Federal Reserve so far has kept nominal interest rates at zero. The experience of the late 1970s in the United States provides some support to the view that once inflation gets even a few percentage points above average, it will then be hard to bring inflation expectations down.

At the same time, an unwillingness to accept higher inflation was one of the policy mistakes that contributed to prolonging the Great Depression and the Japanese slump of the 1990s. Of particular relevance is the US experience in 1937–38. At the start of 1937, the US economy had been recovering from the 1929–33 tumble at a fast pace, leading to optimism that the depression might soon end. Both the administration and the Fed reversed their anticrisis stance and started publicly worrying about the increasing risk of inflation, and newspapers and commentators pointed to the large increase in the monetary base, just as some are doing now. The Fed raised the amount of legally required reserves that banks had to hold in an attempt to contract the money supply, raising nominal interest rates and curbing inflation. In the two years that followed, the United States had one of the sharpest contractions in industrial production in its history. Only when those policies were reversed did the economy start expanding again. By then, however, the damage was done, and it took almost three years to fully recover.

This lesson from history should give serious pause to the Fed if it starts focusing too much on avoiding future inflation when there is little evidence for it. While it is in the nature of central bankers to be conservative and to worry about inflation, during a deep crisis such as the one existing today, all things considered, erring on the side of a loose monetary policy for too long may be the least bad of mistakes.

Finally, the last change as a result of the crisis was the payment of interest on reserves and the more than doubling of the monetary base. This is a change that is dear to academics, since for more than forty years, starting with the work of Milton Friedman, there has been a defense of the current situation as an almost ideal state of affairs. The argument is that money is a good which is created at close to no cost by society: all it takes is a few more digits in electronic records to create additional reserves and an insignificant cost in paper and ink to print currency. Yet, the liquidity it provides is socially useful. It is therefore optimal, from the perspective of society, to flood the economy with liquidity until everyone's demand for it is fully satiated. If this takes many billions of dollars, then so be it.

A related way to make this point is to note that the opportunity cost of money for banks is that they earn only the interest rate on reserves on their holdings of money but could be earning the federal funds rate if they lent it to other banks. If the two interest rates are the same, this opportunity cost disappears. Banks and, going down the chain, households are then effectively satiated in their desire for money, since holding it becomes costless. When the Fed could not pay interest on reserves, this outcome could only be reached when interest rates were zero. This has often been referred to as the "Friedman rule."

Now that interest can be paid on reserves, it is possible to accomplish the Friedman rule by setting that interest rate equal to (or slightly below) the interest rate targeted in the federal funds market. The size of the money supply will then be whatever people happen to demand, now that liquidity is free. It may fluctuate, and even change abruptly over time, but as long as the two interest rates that the Federal Reserve now controls are set the same, this will be inconsequential for inflation. What is important is that there is enough money (or liquidity) in the economy for it not to constrain people's actions unnecessarily.

Conclusion

Changes, especially those that come unexpectedly, bring about worry. After 2008, a deep financial and real crisis in the United States has forced the Fed to make many changes in the conduct of monetary policy. For an institution that prides itself on its conservatism, and where any significant reforms usually follow year-long (or even decade-long) debates, these changes were both unexpected and uncomfortable. Even if they were necessary, it is no surprise that there is already discussion of exit strategies, or ways to reverse all of the changes.

Whether it is possible to go back to the old regime and whether this is desirable are questions whose answers are still tentative. Still, in spite of a few dangers, there are also a few ways out, and with the right combination of skill and luck, US monetary policy may emerge better than it was before.

References

Federal Reserve Bank of Philadelphia. 2009. "Survey of Professional Forecasters." Quarter 4. http://www.phil.frb.org/research-and-data/real-time-center/survey-of-professional-forecasters.

Federal Reserve Economic Data (FRED), Federal Reserve Bank of St. Louis. http://research.stlouisfed.org/fred2.

Federal Reserve Statistical Release. 2010. "H.4.1: Factors Affecting Reserve Balances." January 21. http://www.federalreserve.gov/releases/h41.

Historical Statistics of the United States. Millennial Edition. http://hsus.cambridge.org.

Notes

1. Survey of Professional Forecasters 2009, Quarter 4 Release, Federal Reserve Bank of Philadelphia, November 16, 2009, http://www.phil.frb.org/research-and-data/real-time-center/survey-of-professional-forecasters.

2. As of May 16, 2012, from the Factors Affecting Reserve Balances (H.4.1). Board of Governors of the Federal Reserve.

8

Exits from Recessions: The US Experience, 1920–2007

Michael D. Bordo and John S. Landon-Lane

December 2009 (revised May 2012)

Introduction

The recession of 2007–2009 ended in June 2009, and the US economy has been recovering slowly ever since. Monetary policy has been expansionary since fall 2008 (as has fiscal policy). The Federal Reserve reduced the funds rate from 5.25 percent in August 2007 to close to zero by January 2009, and the Fed has followed two rounds of quantitative easing. There is considerable interest in when the Fed should turn its policy toward one consistent with long-run growth and low inflation—the exit strategy. This involves switching from expansionary to neutral monetary policy, reducing the Fed's balance sheet, and, for fiscal policy, reducing the large fiscal deficits and reducing the national debt.

The key question is when this should happen. A leading view on the issue argues that because of the financial crisis, the credit crunch, and the large overhang of nonperforming loans and toxic assets, the recovery will be slow and the need to tighten will not occur for quite some time. This view is backed up by cross-country evidence, which demonstrates that recessions accompanied by financial turmoil tend to be deeper and longer (Claessens, Kose, and Terrones 2008; Reinhart and Rogoff 2009). An alternative view argues that in US history, deep recessions (including those accompanied by financial crises) have been followed by rapid recoveries (Mussa 2009) and that this recovery may be slow in reflecting deep-seated structural factors

(Stock and Watson 2012) and the collapse of the housing sector (Bordo and Haubrich 2012). These factors may not be easily overcome by continued expansionary monetary policy.

The risks facing monetary policy with respect to the exit strategy are twofold: tightening too soon and creating a double-dip recession, and tightening too late leading to a run-up of inflation. There are a number of famous historical examples of each type of error. Tightening too soon after the Great Contraction led to the recession of 1937–38. Tightening too late in the recessions of the 1960s and 1970s contributed to the Great Inflation.

In this chapter, we examine the historical record of US business cycles from 1920 to 2007. First we provide a brief historical narrative on each of the cycles. Then we present descriptive evidence on the timing of policy change from ease to tightness and on the changes of macro aggregates around the lower turning point of each cycle, based on the work of the National Bureau for Economic Research (NBER). We divide the sample in two: cycles before World War II from 1920 to 1938, and cycles from 1948 to the present.

To supplement the descriptive analysis, we then run some simple regressions of the timing of policy changes relative to the trough of the real variables (real gross national product [GNP], industrial production, the output gap, and unemployment) and price variables (inflation and the price level pre-1960). We also use the coefficients of the effects of the timing of the indicator in the postwar period to predict the possible exits from the current recession.

We can discern some basic patterns from history. In general, in the post–World War II period, the Fed tends to tighten when inflation (the price level) is rising and postpones tightening when the output gap and unemployment have yet to turn. However, the decision to wait until unemployment (the output gap) turns dominates the decision to tighten when inflation rises. The timing of tightening differs somewhat before and after World War II. In the prewar era, the Fed generally tightened when the price level turned up. This policy sometimes caused it to tighten too soon. In the postwar era, the Fed, by focusing on unemployment, tends to err on the side of tightening too late—that is, after inflation resurges.

We also find that there are a few cycles when the Fed got the timing just right and followed a countercyclical policy.[1] These were in the 1920s and

1950s, as discussed by Friedman and Schwartz (1963) and Meltzer (2003, 2010). In most cycles, Fed actions were procyclical.

We further note a significant difference between the cycles before 1965, when the Fed adhered to some form of gold-standard convertibility rule and attached the highest priority to price stability (Bordo and Eichengreen 2008), and the cycles since, when the gold standard became a less important consideration and then did not matter at all. In the late 1960s and 1970s, the Fed generally waited until unemployment and the output gap declined before tightening and placed little emphasis on the pace of inflation. Since the Volcker shock in the early 1980s, the Fed has placed more emphasis on reducing inflation in determining its exit strategy. A memorable episode in which the Fed tightened when unemployment was high and rising was in 1981, when Fed chairman Paul Volcker was determined to break the back of inflation.

In the early 1990s and early 2000s, the Fed, concerned with persistent unemployment ("a jobless recovery"), waited too long. In the first case, significant tightening occurred close to three years after the trough following the inflation scare of 1994. In the second case, the Fed, concerned with the risk of deflation, waited four years after the trough and accordingly may have ignited the housing-price boom that burst in 2006 leading to the 2007–2009 recession.

Historical Narrative: 1920–38

Peak January 1920; Trough July 1921. The recession of 1920–21 was one of the three worst recessions of the twentieth century. Friedman and Schwartz (1963) viewed it as the Fed's first policy failure. They indicted the Fed for waiting too long to raise rates to stem the inflationary boom that followed World War I, and then for waiting too long to reverse the ensuing recession. The Fed waited until November 1919 to begin tightening because the Treasury pressured the Fed to keep the prices of its wartime bond issues high. During the recession that followed, real GNP fell by 15 percent, industrial production (IP) fell by 23 percent, the GNP deflator fell by 20 percent, and the unemployment rate increased by 8 percent.

The cause of the recession was the Fed's decision (triggered by a decline in its gold reserves) to implement a rapid deflation to roll back the run-up in prices that had occurred since the United States entered World War I. The Fed raised the discount rate from 4.75 percent in January 1920 to 7 percent in June and kept it at that level until May 1921. The highly persistent rise in nominal interest rates in the face of a shift in expectations from inflation to deflation represented a much tighter policy stance than agents anticipated (Bordo et al. 2007). In the face of mounting political pressure, the Fed reversed course four months after the recession ended. IP recovered in August and by March 1922 had increased 20 percent above the previous year.

Peak May 1923; Trough July 1924. The recession of 1923–24 was relatively brief and, by pre–World War II standards, mild: real GNP fell by 4 percent. The recession followed a tightening of monetary policy beginning in May 1922, which reflected concern that the rapid recovery from the previous recession was becoming inflationary. In contrast to the previous recession, the Fed began reversing course soon after the recession became apparent in December 1923, with open market operations and then cuts in the discount rate in May 1924 (Meltzer 2003). Friedman and Schwartz (1963) gave the Fed high marks for conducting a successful countercyclical policy.

Peak October 1926; Trough November 1927. Similar to the recession of 1923–24, the Fed began tightening, reflecting fears of inflation, in January 1925, with open market sales and then a rise in the discount rate in February. As in the preceding recession, the Fed reversed course and began open market purchases in May 1927, halfway through the mild recession (Meltzer 2003).

Peak August 1929; Trough March 1933. The Great Contraction of 1929–33, during which prices, real GNP, and the money stock (M2) declined by about a third, was the worst recession in US history. Since Friedman and Schwartz (1963), it is widely attributed to policy failures at the Federal Reserve. Beginning in 1927, the Federal Reserve Board became increasingly concerned over stock market speculation and the growing boom on Wall Street. Based on the real bills doctrine, many officials believed that stock market speculation was inflationary. The Fed began monetary restraint with open market sales in February 1928 and continued this policy through 1929, with a rise in the discount rate from 5 to 6 percent in August 1929.

The tightening, while insufficient to halt the stock market boom, was sufficient to induce a downturn beginning in August 1929. The stock market crash in October 1929 exacerbated the downturn but did not cause the depression. The failure of the Fed to follow its mandate from the Federal Reserve Act of 1913 to act as a lender of last resort and to allay a series of four banking panics beginning in October 1930 led to the serious downturn that followed. A major hike in the discount rate in October 1931 designed to protect the dollar after sterling's exit from the gold standard added fuel to the fire. Despite short-lived expansionary open market purchases in spring 1932, which, if continued, could have ended the recession (Friedman and Schwartz 1963), the recovery in March 1933 was not precipitated by Fed policy.

Recovery began in March 1933 with President Franklin D. Roosevelt's banking holiday, ending the fourth banking panic. The country's banks were closed for a week, during which an army of bank inspectors separated the insolvent banks from the rest. Insolvent banks were closed, ending the uncertainty driving the panic. This action was quickly followed by Roosevelt taking the United States off the gold standard in April 1933, Treasury gold (and silver) purchases designed to raise gold prices and prices in general, and formal devaluation of the dollar by close to 60 percent in January 1934. These policies produced a big reflationary impulse from gold inflows, which were passing unsterilized directly into the money supply. They also helped convert deflationary expectations into inflationary ones (Eggertsson 2008).

The recovery of 1933 to 1941 was largely driven by gold inflows, initially reflecting Treasury policies and the devaluation, later reflecting capital flight from Europe as war loomed. Expansionary fiscal policy played only a minor role in the recovery of the 1930s (Romer 1992). Recovery was impeded somewhat by New Deal cartelization policies like the National Industrial Recovery Act, which artificially reduced labor supply and aggregate supply in an attempt to raise wages and prices (Cole and Ohanian 2004). Over the period 1933–37, output increased by 33 percent.

Peak May 1937; Trough June 1938. The 1937–38 recession, which cut short the rapid recovery from the Great Contraction of 1929–33, was the third-worst recession in the twentieth century: real GNP declined by 10 percent, and unemployment, which had declined considerably after 1933, increased to 20 percent. The recession was primarily a consequence of a serious policy mistake by the Fed. Mounting concern by the Fed over the inflationary consequences of the buildup in excess reserves in member banks (held as a precaution against a repeat of the banking panics of the early 1930s) led the Board of Governors to double reserve requirements in three steps between August 1936 and May 1937. Fed officials were concerned that these reserves would lead to an explosion of lending and would foster a reoccurrence of the asset-price speculation of the 1920s. They also believed that reducing excess reserves would encourage member banks to borrow at the discount window. The Burgess-Riefler doctrine that prevailed at the time argued that the Fed could exert monetary control by using open market operations to affect member bank borrowing and hence to alter bank lending (Meltzer 2003).

The consequence of doubling reserve requirements was that banks sold off their earning assets and cut their lending to restore their desired cushion of precautionary reserves. The Fed's contractionary policy action was complemented by the Treasury's decision in late 1936 to sterilize gold inflows in order to reduce excess reserves. These policy actions led to a spike in short-term interest rates and a severe decline in money supply.

The recession ended in April 1938 after Roosevelt pressured the Fed to roll back reserve requirements, the Treasury stopped sterilizing gold inflows and desterilized all the remaining gold sterilized since December 1936, and the administration began pursuing expansionary fiscal policy. The recovery from 1938 to 1942 was spectacular; output grew by 49 percent, fueled by gold inflows from Europe and a major defense buildup.

Peak November 1948; Trough October 1949. After the war, inflation increased to 15 percent per year by 1948. Tightening by both the Treasury and the Fed began in October 1947. A mild recession ensued beginning in November 1948. Real GNP fell by less than 2 percent, IP by 9 percent, and Consumer Price Index (CPI) prices by 2 percent. Fed policy was slow to change during the recession because the Fed viewed low nominal interest rates (T bills) at close to 1 percent as evidence of ease and did not realize that real rates were elevated in the face of recession. The board reduced reserve requirements by 2 percent in May 1949. According to Meltzer (2003, chapter 7), 1948–49 was similar to 1920–21 in that deflation—by both encouraging gold inflows and increasing the real value of the monetary base—helped to reinflate the economy.

Peak July 1953; Trough May 1954. After the Federal Reserve–Treasury Accord of March 1951, the Fed was again free to use its policy rates to pursue its policy aims. One of the first occasions was at the end of the Korean War, when both monetary and fiscal policy tightened to prevent an increase in inflation. In January 1953, the Fed raised its discount rate and the real money base declined, leading to a recession beginning in July. The real economy declined by 3.2 percent, IP declined by 9.4 percent, and unemployment rose to 6.1 percent. However, unlike earlier recessions, the Fed eased policy in June 1953 to offset a spike in long-term Treasury bond rates. Ease continued with a decline in reserve requirements in July 1953; a decline in the discount rate in February, April, and May 1954; and declines in reserve requirements in June and July. By October 1954, with recovery well underway, the Fed began to tighten in December in the face of incipient inflationary pressure. The Fed raised the discount rate in seven steps from the end of 1954 to 1957. This was evident in a rise in ex post interest rates (Meltzer 2010, chapter 2; Friedman and Schwartz 1963, chapter 11).

Peak August 1957; Trough April 1958. Growing concern over the pace of recovery from the previous recession and a run-up in inflation in 1955 led the Fed to begin tightening in April by raising the discount rate. Further increases followed in 1956. The ensuing recession was relatively mild, with real GNP falling by 3 percent and unemployment rising to 7.5 percent. The Fed was slow to respond to the recession because of continuing concern over inflation (Meltzer 2010, chapter 2). It began easing in November 1957 by reducing the discount rate and reserve requirements and conducting open market purchases in March and April 1958. The recovery was vigorous, and the Fed, again worried about inflation, began tightening (raising the discount rate) in August, four months after the trough. It was also concerned for the first time in the postwar period with gold outflows (Friedman and Schwartz 1963, 618).

Peak April 1960; Trough February 1961. The Fed began tightening in spring 1959 in the face of rising inflation and gold outflows. By early 1960, the Federal Reserve Board's policy-setting group, the Federal Open Market Committee (FOMC), recognized that the economy had slowed and began to ease two months before the April business-cycle peak, as it had done in 1953. The ensuing recession was mild and lasted ten months. Real GNP fell by less than 1 percent, and unemployment increased to 7 percent. Fed policy continued to be loose throughout the downturn: the discount rate was cut in March and August and reserve requirements were cut in August. The recession ended in February. After the trough, the policy directive for ease was moderated in April (Meltzer 2010, chapter 3). The real federal funds rate began to rise one quarter after the trough, and the growth of the real base slowed at the trough. Unemployment peaked in May.

Peak November 1969; Trough November 1970. The period from 1961 to 1964 exhibited rapid growth with low inflation. Inflation began to rise in 1965. The Fed tightened in December 1965 against President Lyndon B. Johnson's wishes, but not enough to stem rising inflation. Further tightening in spring and summer 1966 led to the credit crunch of 1966, a growth slowdown but not a recession (Bordo and Haubrich 2009). The Fed began tightening again in summer 1969, seen in a decline in real base growth and a rise in real interest rates leading to the mild recession that began in July 1969. Real GNP fell less than half a percent, unemployment increased to 5.9 percent, and inflation only slowed moderately. Policy began to ease after January 1970, seen in a flattening of real base growth.

In April 1970, Fed chairman Arthur Burns abandoned the anti-inflationary policy that had been pursued by his predecessor, William McChesney Martin, because of the slowing economy. By June 1970, real base growth was positive and real interest rates declined. The easy policies continued until after the trough. Recovery in real GNP was relatively sluggish, and unemployment did not peak until summer 1971. Policy shifted to less ease after the trough, seen in a rise in the real funds rate and a flattening of real growth. This recession was the first during the Great Inflation episode in which the Fed revealed its unwillingness to stem inflation at the expense of unemployment (Meltzer 2010, chapter 3).

Peak November 1973; Trough March 1975. The Nixon administration imposed wage-price controls in August 1971 to fight unemployment, but the policy was unsuccessful. CPI inflation increased to 10 percent by 1974. In the face of rising inflation from December to August 1972, the Fed tightened, but not enough (Meltzer 2010, chapter 6). Further tightening occurred in summer 1973, seen in a decline in real base growth. The recession, which began in November, was one of the worst in the postwar period: real GNP declined by 4.7 percent and unemployment increased to 8.6 percent. The recession was greatly aggravated by the first oil price shock, which doubled the price of oil and, by the price controls, prevented the necessary adjustment. Beginning in July 1974, the Fed shifted to easier policy in the face of rising unemployment, seen in a reversal in the federal funds rate (both nominal and real). Monetary ease continued in the first quarter of 1975 when the Fed cut the funds rate, the discount rate, and reserve requirements. The recovery began in April 1975, but according to Meltzer (2010, chapter 7), the Fed did not recognize it until August. The Fed, still concerned with inflation, began increasing the funds rate in the quarter after the recession ended, and real base growth flattened in the same quarter.

Peak January 1980; Trough July 1980. By 1979, inflation had reached double-digit levels. In August 1979, President Jimmy Carter appointed a well-known inflation hawk, Paul Volcker, as chairman of the Federal Reserve. Two months after taking office, Volcker announced a major shift in policy aimed at rapidly lowering the inflation rate. He desired the policy change to be interpreted as a decisive break from past policies that had allowed the run-up in inflation. The announcement was followed by a series of sizable hikes in the federal funds rate. The roughly 7 percentage point rise in the nominal funds rate between October 1979 and April 1980 was the largest increase over a six-month period in the history of the Federal Reserve System. The tight monetary stance was temporarily abandoned in mid-1980 as interest rates spiked and economic activity decelerated sharply. The FOMC then imposed credit controls (March to July 1980) and let the funds rate decline—moves that the Carter administration had politically supported. The controls led to a marked decline in consumer credit, personal consumption, and economic activity, leading to an increase in unemployment from 6.3 to 7.5 percent. In July 1980, the Fed shifted to an expansionary monetary policy, seen in cuts in the federal funds rate and increases in real base growth. The recession ended in July 1980, followed by a rapid recovery. Fed policy started to tighten again in May 1981 in the face of a jump in inflation, seen in a sharp reversal in real base growth and then successive rises in the discount rate beginning in September. The FOMC policy reversal and acquiescence to political pressure in 1980 were widely viewed as a signal that it was not committed to achieving a sustained fall in inflation. Having failed to convince price and wage setters that inflation was going to fall, the GNP deflator rose almost 10 percent in 1980.

Peak July 1981; Trough November 1982. The Fed embarked on a new round of tightening in spring 1981. It raised the federal funds rate from 14.7 percent in March to 19.1 percent in June. This second and more durable round of tightening succeeded in reducing the inflation rate from about 10 percent in early 1981 to about 4 percent in 1983, but at the cost of a sharp and prolonged recession. Real GNP fell by close to 5 percent, and unemployment increased from 7.2 percent to 10.8 percent. The Fed's tightening during a recession was initially supported by both President Ronald Reagan and Congress. However, by spring 1982, the Fed faced increasing pressure from Congress and the administration to loosen policy. There was also concern over the solvency of the money center banks hit by the Latin American debt defaults and over the effects of high interest rates on other countries. The Fed shifted to a looser policy in June 1982, with a decline in the discount rate and the federal funds rate and a rise in the growth rate of the real monetary base. After the trough, real output, the output gap, and IP rose rapidly. Unemployment peaked quickly. Policy tightened somewhat in terms of both the real funds rate and the real base soon after the trough, reflecting the FOMC's determination to continue to reduce inflation (Meltzer 2010, chapter 8).

Peak July 1990; Trough March 1991. The recession of 1991 was preceded by Fed tightening beginning in December 1988 (Romer and Romer 1994). The FOMC wanted to reduce inflation from the 4–4.5 percent range. The federal funds rate rose from 6.5 percent to 9.9 percent between March 1988 and May 1989. The recession began in July 1990 and was aggravated by an oil price shock after Iraq invaded Kuwait in August 1990. The recession was mild. Real GNP fell by only 1.4 percent. The FOMC only began cutting the federal funds rate in November because its primary concern was to reduce inflation, which had reached 6.1 percent in the first half of 1990 (Hetzel 2008, chapter 15).

The recovery from the trough in March 1991 was considered tepid (real output grew at 3.6 percent for the three years following the trough, compared to the postwar average of 5 percent), and it was referred to as a jobless recovery—unemployment peaked at 7.7 percent in June 1992.The recession is also viewed as a credit crunch (Bernanke and Lown 1991). Evidence in Bordo and Haubrich (2009) and the International Monetary Fund *World Economic Outlook* (2008) suggests that recessions involving credit events tend to last longer. The federal funds rate declined until October 1992. Inflation began to pick up in the first quarter of 1993, and by early 1994 the Fed shifted to a tighter policy, the inflation scare of 1994 (Hetzel 2008, 202).

Peak March 2001; Trough November 2001. In 2000, the Fed loosened monetary policy because of the fear of Y2K. The tech boom, which had elevated the NASDAQ to unsustainable levels, burst, leading to a decline in wealth and consumption. The FOMC did not forecast a recession and was slow to respond because of tightness in the labor market (Hetzel 2008, 241). Although real growth began decelerating in mid-2000, the FOMC began reducing the funds rate in January 2001 and lowered the rate from 6.5 to 1 percent by June 2003. Real short-term rates fell from 5 percent in mid-2001 to zero percent in mid-2002, but not rapidly enough to prevent policy from being contractionary (Hetzel 2008, 242). Although real growth had picked up after the trough in November, employment had not, and like the previous recession, there was talk about a jobless recovery. By March 2004, the unemployment rate was at 5.7 percent, still near its cyclical peak. Moreover, the Fed worried about deflation and the zero-lower-bound problem in 2003. Consequently, the federal funds rate was maintained at its recession low until June 2004, when alarm caused by an increase in inflationary expectations led the Fed to begin raising the federal funds rate in 0.25 percent increments until late summer 2007.

Peak December 2007; Trough June 2009. The recent recession is familiar in some respects and novel in others. It is familiar in that the recession, although somewhat longer in duration and somewhat deeper than the postwar average, is within the realm of the postwar experience. It is novel in that it was precipitated by a financial crisis caused by the end of a major housing boom. It has been argued by many that a key contributing factor to the asset boom, along with lax regulatory oversight and a relaxation of normal standards of prudent lending, was an extended period of loose monetary policy from 2002 to 2004 in reaction to slow employment growth, fears of incipient crises, and deflation. Contributing factors to the asset bust include a return to tighter monetary policy in 2005, the collapse of the subprime mortgage market, and the debunking of the securitization model by which derivatives, including toxic mortgages, were bundled. The severity of the resultant recession, from December 2007 to summer 2009, reflected both a credit crunch and tight Federal Reserve policies in 2008, seen in high real federal funds rates (Hetzel 2009). The recession is in some respects the most severe event in the postwar period (real GNP declined by close to 4 percent and unemployment reached 10 percent), and the financial crisis is without doubt the most serious event since the Great Depression (the quality spread, as measured by the spread between the yield on BAA-rated commercial debt and the yield on long-term Treasury debt, increased by 342 basis points by April 2009, which was higher than in 1929–33).

Both the crisis and the recession were dealt with by vigorous policy responses (expansionary monetary policy cutting the funds rate from 5.25 percent in early fall 2007 to close to zero by January 2009 and a massive fiscal stimulus package), by unorthodox quantitative easing (the purchase of mortgage-backed securities and long-term Treasuries since January 2009), and by an extensive network of facilities (such as the Term Auction Facility) created to support the credit market directly and reduce spreads (involving a tripling of the Fed's balance sheet). It is too soon to analyze the recovery or the exit strategy, but in a subsequent section we use our econometric analysis to estimate when tightening will occur.

Using historical narratives allowed us to determine those exits in which the Fed was deemed to have exited too early, too late, or at the right time. We next turn to a more descriptive analysis, where we analyze the patterns between the turning points of the policy variables and the turning points of the real and nominal variables that we follow.

Turning Point Analysis

For all the business cycles since 1920 (excluding the two cycles that brack-eted World War II), we ascertained the turning points in the quarterly val-ues of several policy variables: before 1954, the discount rate (nominal and real); since 1954, the federal funds rate (nominal and real); the growth rate of the monetary base (nominal and real); and the growth rate of M2 money stock (nominal and real). We did the same for several real macro-aggregates: real GNP, industrial production, the unemployment rate, the output gap, and two measures of the price level and inflation (the GNP deflator and the CPI).[2] For data sources and definitions, see appendix table 8-A1.

In the period before 1960, when inflation was generally low and the United States adhered to some form of the gold standard (under which prices are mean reverting), we focus on the price level as a policy target. Since 1960, inflation has been continuously positive, so we focus on mea-sures of inflation as our policy target.

Determining the Turning Points. The turning points of each of the series, reported in tables 8-1 and 8-2 below, were determined as follows: for each of the macroeconomic aggregate variables (two measures of the price level and inflation, real output, industrial production, the output gap, and unem-ployment), the date at which the variable started to improve after the start of the recession was chosen by visual inspection of the time series figures for each variable as shown in the appendix.

For the price level and inflation, this was the first date after the start of the recession when the price level or inflation rate changed from having a negative slope to a positive slope. Similarly, for real output, industrial pro-duction, and the output gap, we looked for the first quarter after the start of the recession in which the slope of the series changed from being negative to positive. The rule for unemployment was the opposite, with the turning point being the first quarter after the start of the recession in which the derivative of the unemployment series changed from positive to negative.

For the policy variables, the decision rule was to look for the first period in which there is evidence of monetary tightening. For the various interest rate series, this meant looking for the first quarter after the start of the recession in which interest rates started to increase from a period of

TABLE 8-1a

DESCRIPTIVE EVIDENCE POLICY VARIABLES, 1920–1937

Cycle	Narra- tives	Discount Rate	Real Discount Rate	Base Growth	Real Base Growth	M2 Growth	Real M2 Growth
1. 1920Q1–1923Q1 (1921Q3)[a]	3[b]	5	—	5	1	2	2
2. 1923Q2–1926Q2 (1924Q3)	3	1	2	0	2	−1	2
3. 1926Q3–1929Q2 (1927Q4)	1	0	0	1	0	0	0
4. 1929Q3–1937Q1 (1933Q1)	14	—	—	3	3	−2	4

SOURCE: Authors' calculations.

[a] Numbers in parentheses are the NBER trough dates for each cycle.

[b] Numbers in cells represent number of quarters after official NBER trough date that the series was determined to have turned. In the case of the policy variables, this was the date of initial tightening. Missing values represent a cycle in which no definitive turning point was identified.

TABLE 8-1b

DESCRIPTIVE EVIDENCE MACRO AGGREGATES, 1920–1937

Cycle	Price Level (GNP defl.)	Price Level (CPI)	Real GNP	Industrial Produc- tion	Output Gap	Unem- ployment
1. 1920Q1–1923Q1 (1921Q3)[a]	3[b]	2	−2	−2	−2	−2
2. 1923Q2–1926Q2 (1924Q3)	0	−2	0	−1	0	−2
3. 1926Q3–1929Q2 (1927Q4)	−2	1	0	0	0	1
4. 1929Q3–1937Q1 (1933Q1)	0	0	0	0	0	−4

SOURCE: Authors' calculations.

[a] Numbers in parentheses are the NBER trough dates for each cycle.

[b] Numbers in cells represent number of quarters after official NBER trough date that the series was determined to have turned. In the case of the policy variables, this was the date of initial tightening.

TABLE 8-2a

DESCRIPTIVE EVIDENCE POLICY VARIABLES, 1948–2007

Cycle	Narra-tives	Federal Funds Rate (Dis-count Rate)	Real Federal Funds Rate (Real Discount Rate)	Base Growth	Real Base Growth	M2 Growth	Real M2 Growth
1. 1948Q4–1953Q1 (1949Q4)[a]	−2[b]	(2)	(6)	−2	−2	1	0
2. 1953Q2–1957Q2 (1954Q2)	3	2	1	1	1	0	0
3. 1957Q3–1960Q1 (1958Q2)	1	0	0	−1	−1	−1	−1
4. 1960Q2–1969Q3 (1961Q1)	1	1	2	2	2	0	−1
5. 1969Q4–1973Q3 (1970Q4)	1	1	1	0	−2	1	1
6. 1973Q4–1979Q4 (1975Q1)	0	1	0	0	0	0	0
7. 1980Q1–1981Q2 (1980Q3)	3	0	0	−1	−1	−1	−1
8. 1981Q3–1990Q2 (1982Q4)	3	1	−1	0	1	0	0
9. 1990Q3–2000Q4 (1991Q1)	12	9	9	5	5	−1	0
10. 2001Q1–2007Q3 (2001Q4)	10	10	5	0	0	3	−1

SOURCE: Authors' calculations.

[a] Numbers in parentheses are the NBER trough dates for each cycle.

[b] Numbers in cells represent number of quarters after official NBER trough date that the series was determined to have turned. In the case of the policy variables, this was the date of initial tightening.

falling or relatively level rates. For the monetary aggregate growth variables, we looked for the first quarter after the start of the recession in which the aggregate growth rates started to fall from a time of increasing growth rates or relatively constant growth rates.

Obviously this approach of visual inspection is a subjective approach to selecting turning points of time series, but in almost all cases, there was a

TABLE 8-2b
DESCRIPTIVE EVIDENCE MACRO AGGREGATES, 1948–2007

Cycle	Inflation (GNP) (Price Level)	Inflation (CPI) (Price Level)	Real GNP	Industrial Production	Output Gap	Unemployment
1. 1948Q4–1953Q1 (1949Q4)[a]	0(1)[b]	–2(1)	0	–2	0	0
2. 1953Q2–1957Q2 (1954Q2)	0(–2)	1(2)	–1	–1	0	1
3. 1957Q3–1960Q1 (1958Q2)	–1	0	–1	–1	0	0
4. 1960Q2–1969Q3 (1961Q1)	–1	0	–1	–1	0	1
5. 1969Q4–1973Q3 (1970Q4)	–2	0	0	0	0	3
6. 1973Q4–1979Q4 (1975Q1)	0	0	0	0	0	1
7. 1980Q1–1981Q2 (1980Q3)	–1	–1	0	–1	0	0
8. 1981Q3–1990Q2 (1982Q4)	1	0	–1	0	0	0
9. 1990Q3–2000Q4 (1991Q1)	5	0	0	0	2	6
10. 2001Q1–2007Q3 (2001Q4)	–1	–1	–1	0	5	7

SOURCE: Authors' calculations.

[a] Numbers in parentheses are the NBER trough dates for each cycle.

[b] Numbers in cells represent number of quarters after official NBER trough date that the series was determined to have turned. In the case of the policy variables, this was the date of initial tightening.

clear-cut choice. In some cases, there seemed to be multiple periods close together that could be considered a turning point of a series. In these cases, we made sure to pick a turning point where there were at least two quarters on each side of the turning point where the time series was either always above or always below the level of the series, depending on the type of series being inspected. In the rare cases where there were multiple turning points that did not meet these criteria, we chose the turning point that was the highest or lowest point depending on the type of series. In the case of the policy variables, if there was any doubt about the turning point, we chose the turning point closest to the date of the turning point inferred by our reading of the historical narratives above.

Descriptive Evidence. Appendix tables 8-A2a and 8-A2b display the dates of the turning points. In tables 8-1 and 8-2, we present the timing of turning points of a data series as the number of quarters the turning point of the series occurred after the NBER trough (a minus sign indicates number of quarters before the trough.)

Table 8-1 shows the timing of the turning points relative to the NBER trough of the policy variables and the macro aggregates for each cycle in the pre–World War II period (1920–1937). Table 8-2 shows the timing of the turning points relative to the NBER trough from the cycles from 1948 to 2007. In both tables, we also show the timing of tightening as discerned from the historical narratives above.

Pre–World War II: 1920–1937. In this narrative, we briefly describe the salient patterns of the policy indicators and the real aggregates and prices.

- **1920Q1–1923Q1; Trough 1921Q3.** In this cycle, the official discount rate tightened well after the trough, after the real aggregates, and after the price level turned up. Policy measured by the growth in the real monetary base and by real M2 also tightened after the NBER trough and after the real aggregates (real GNP, IP, the output gap, and unemployment) turned but before the price level increased. Thus, in this cycle, policy measured by real base growth was relatively well timed to prevent rising prices, but measured by the discount rate, the Fed was too late.

- **1923Q2–1926Q2; Trough 1924Q3.** In this cycle, monetary policy (both the official discount rate and the real rate in addition to real base growth) tightened after the real economy turned up and after the price level turned up. This suggests that policy was too late to prevent prices from rising.

- **1926Q3–1929Q2; Trough 1927Q4.** Monetary policy (with the exception of base growth) tightened when the real economy turned up and before the CPI price level (but after the GNP deflator) turned. This suggests that policy was more or less on time.

- **1929Q3–1937Q1; Trough 1933Q1.** The Great Contraction ended in March 1933. Policy tightened long after recovery began, based on the monetary aggregates. The Fed rarely changed its policy rates from 1934 to 1951, since it was subservient to the Treasury for most of this period and was committed to maintaining a low interest rate peg. This suggests that the nominal discount rate is not a good measure of the stance of policy. Significant tightening after this trough occurred in 1936, according to the narratives, when the Fed began doubling reserve requirements (although the monetary aggregates in table 8-1 show minor slowdowns in 1933–34). The doubling of reserve requirements occurred after real economic activity and prices turned up, but well before output reached full capacity and while unemployment was still high. This episode is generally viewed as one where policy tightened too soon.

Post–World War II, 1948–2007. We omitted the two cycles containing the war years from the analysis. In these cycles—1937Q2–1944Q4; Trough 1938Q2 and 1945Q1–1948Q3; Trough 1945Q4—the timing of monetary policy changes seemed unconnected to the business cycle and occurred many years after the troughs. This made it difficult to analyze the timing of the exit from recession comparable to the peacetime cycles.

- **1948Q4–1953Q1; Trough 1949Q4.** In this first postwar cycle, the discount rate (nominal and real) tightened after the real economy recovered and after inflation (prices) turned up. Real and nominal base growth turned up before the real economy, with CPI, and before GNP inflation.

- **1953Q2–1957Q2; Trough 1954Q2.** Monetary policy measured by the federal funds rate (nominal and real) began tightening, not immediately after real GNP began to recover but when unemployment peaked. Policy tightened after GNP inflation (prices) picked up but before the CPI. As measured by real base growth, monetary policy was too late for GNP inflation (prices) but just about on time for CPI inflation (prices). This suggests that, on average, monetary policy was close to being timely.

- **1957Q3–1960Q1; Trough 1958Q2.** Monetary policy measured by the federal funds rate (real and nominal) suggests that tightening occurred after the real economy turned but at the same time as unemployment and the output gap turned and before GNP inflation turned up. By this measure, policy was just right. Moreover, real base growth turned close to the real economy and before GNP inflation increased. Again, as in the preceding cycle, the timing of policy was, on average, close to being just right.

- **1960Q2–1969Q3; Trough 1961Q1.** Policy measured by the federal funds rate (nominal and real) turned up close to or after the real economy recovered. The case is similar for inflation. Real base growth turned up after the real economy troughed and after inflation turned up. This was the cycle in which inflation began to rise persistently as discussed above.

- **1969Q4–1973Q3; Trough 1970Q4.** Policy, using both rates and aggregates, tightened after the real economy recovered but was closer to the turning point in unemployment. Moreover, as has been the case in most cycles, policy was procyclical. In addition, policy using both rates and aggregates tightened after GNP inflation picked up. Monetary policy was clearly too late.

- **1973Q4–1979Q4; Trough 1975Q3.** Both measures of policy (the real and nominal funds rate and the nominal and real monetary base) tightened approximately when the real economy began to recover and when inflation turned up. Although the Fed timed its exit well, inflation was not substantially reduced.

- **1980Q1–1981Q2; Trough 1980Q3.** In this cycle, both measures of policy tightened close to when the economy began to recover and shortly after GNP inflation picked up. In this episode, as mentioned above, Fed tightening focusing on monetary aggregates was designed to break the back of inflationary expectations.

- **1981Q3–1990Q2; Trough 1982Q4.** Monetary policy measured by the real and nominal federal funds rate tightened about the time the real economy began to recover and when inflation turned up. A similar pattern holds for nominal and real base growth. Thus, on average, policy was well timed.

- **1990Q3–2000Q4; Trough 1991Q1.** Using the federal funds rate shows that policy tightened after unemployment peaked— six quarters after real activity began recovering. It also tightened after inflation resurged. Using real base growth as a policy measure leads to a similar outcome. Both policy indicators suggest that the Fed was focused on unemployment (the jobless recovery). With respect to stemming inflationary pressure, the Fed was too late.

- **2001Q1–2007Q3; Trough 2001Q4.** Using the nominal funds rate suggests that policy tightened well after GNP recovered and closer to when unemployment began recovering. Both measures tightened long after inflation picked up. These actions suggest that policy tightened too late. The timing of real base growth suggests that the Fed tightened after the real recovery and well before the peak in unemployment but after the turning point in inflation. Using this measure, policy was also too late.

Lessons from the Timing Exercise

The Pre–World War II Evidence. The first lesson is that the pre–World War II evidence suggests that the Fed was too late in tightening to offset incipient inflation more often than not. However, in two episodes (after the recessions of 1921 and 1927), the timing of the policy exit was much better. Second, the verdict on timing often differs between focusing on nominal and real base growth and focusing on the nominal and real discount rates. Meltzer (2003) provides evidence that real base growth is generally more closely lined up with the turning points in the business cycle than is the real discount rate. He also points out that Fed officials did not understand the distinction between nominal and real interest rates.

The Post–World War II Evidence. The first lesson is that, in the postwar cycles, the descriptive evidence suggests that policy was often too late by one measure or another to prevent inflation from rising. The Fed generally tightened when unemployment peaked and when the other real indicators troughed at roughly the same time. However, the recessions of the 1950s stand out as ones where the exit timing was favorable. Second, during the Great Inflation cycles of the 1960s and 1970s, the problem of mistiming the exits was less serious than the unwillingness to tighten sufficiently to stem inflationary pressures. This was not the case after the 1980 recession. Third, in the subsequent Great Moderation period from the mid-1980s to 2007, policy was too late in exiting in the last two cycles of the early 1990s and early 2000s. In each case, monetary policy only tightened when unemployment and the output gap declined, long after the recovery of real activity and a recovery in inflation. However, the Fed's actions in these cycles may reflect the fact that it felt it had achieved credibility for low inflation after its success in stemming inflationary expectations in the 1980s; hence, it felt it could afford to wait. In the last cycle, the Fed was concerned with deflation from 2002 to 2004, and for that reason was reluctant to tighten. The recent recession, with unemployment high, may be similar to the last two episodes in the timing of the exit from monetary ease.

Figure 8-1 summarizes the evidence on tightening in the post–World War II cycles. In each subfigure, the vertical axis shows the number of quarters that the two principal recession variables (unemployment and inflation) turned before the particular policy variable tightened. On the horizontal axis of each subfigure is the year in which the recession ended. A value of –1, for example, means that the recession variable turned one quarter before the Federal Reserve tightened. A positive number means that the variables turned after the policy variable tightened. In all subfigures the 0 line represents the quarter that the tightening occurred for the variable represented in the figure.

In figure 8-1, we report the turning points of unemployment and inflation relative to the tightening dates of five important policy variables: a) the historical narratives, b) the nominal federal funds rate, c) the real federal funds rate, d) the growth rate of the nominal money base, and e) the growth rate of the real money base. Except for the recession ending in 1990, the unemployment line is always above the inflation line, which implies that, except for that one recession, unemployment always turned after inflation. However, the relative position of the turning points to the date of tightening varies by policy variable.

FIGURE 8-1

COMPARISON OF TURNING POINTS FOR UNEMPLOYMENT AND
INFLATION WITH TIGHTENING DATES

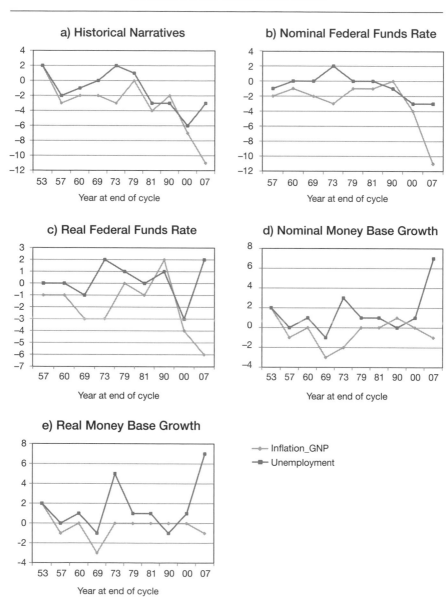

SOURCE: Authors' calculations.

For the historical narratives and the nominal federal funds rate (see the first two subfigures on the first row of figure 8-1), the lines lie almost always below or on the zero line (the date that the policy variable tightened). According to the historical narratives, the Fed tightened after or on the date of the turning point of inflation for all but the recession ending in 1953. In the two recessions that ended in the 1970s, the Federal Reserve tightened before unemployment turned. Other than that, the narratives suggest that the Federal Reserve waited for unemployment to turn before tightening monetary policy. The second subfigure, which looks at the nominal federal funds rate, tells a similar story. The Federal Reserve waited until inflation and unemployment turned before tightening monetary policy. In one case, the most recent complete recession, the Federal Reserve waited a long time for unemployment to turn before tightening monetary policy. In only one case, the recession ending in 1973, did the federal funds rate increase before unemployment turned.

Using the real federal funds rate to identify the tightening date, we observe that, for the early cycles (that is, up until the cycle ending in 1969), the Fed waited for unemployment to turn. During the 1970s, the real federal funds rate tightened before unemployment and after inflation and again during the last complete post–World War II cycle.

For the other nominal policy variable—the growth rate of the monetary base—the pattern is not as obvious. It appears that, with respect to the monetary base, the Fed typically did not wait for unemployment to peak before tightening, but still often tightened after inflation turned up. This is most apparent for the last complete post–World War II recession, in which the tightening occurred seven quarters before unemployment turned, but one quarter after inflation turned.

Finally, looking at the growth rate of the real monetary base series, the pattern shows some similarity to that of the nominal monetary base, but there are two cycles (the cycles ending in 1973 and 2007) for which the real monetary base tightened well before unemployment turned. Also, policy usually tightened close to when unemployment turned, but before inflation turned, and tightening for inflation was often closer to the business cycle trough.

Figure 8-1 shows that across the different policy measures, policy typically tightened close to when unemployment peaked and close to when, but more often after, inflation turned up. This was most evident when we used either the tightening dates suggested by the historical narratives or ones suggested by the key policy variable (the federal funds rate). This highlights the conclusion that policy tightening was often too late to prevent inflation from rising.

Evidence from Simple Regression Analysis

The evidence presented in the section above relied on informally sifting through each recession and the historical narratives to categorize the recessions in our sample. In this section, we aim to use regression analysis to see if there are any systematic relationships between the turning points of the policy variables and the turning points of the recession variables.[3] There have been sixteen full recessions since 1920. As explained above, we do not include the two recessions between 1937Q2 and 1948Q3. Thus, we are left with fourteen recessions. Furthermore, we suspect that the post–World War II recessions may be different from the pre–World War II recessions, so for the postwar sample we are left with only ten recessions. Clearly, there are not enough observations to perform an extensive regression analysis. However, we believe there are enough observations to allow for any systematic relationships between the turning points in the policy variables and the turning points in the recession variables to appear in simple regression models.

In our analysis, we perform two types of regressions. The first is a simple linear regression that aims to see if there is a systematic relationship between the turning point of a policy variable and the turning point of an explanatory variable. For example, we would like to see if there is a relationship between the turning point in unemployment and the turning point in the main policy interest rate—the federal funds rate after 1954 and the nominal discount rate before 1954. For the policy variables, we measure the turning point as the first quarter after the start of the recession in which the Federal Reserve began to pursue tighter monetary policy. For the recession variables—that is, the variables that reflect the current state of the economy—we record the turning point as the first quarter after the start of the recession in which that variable started to improve. For example, in the case of unemployment, this would be the quarter in which the unemployment rate started to decline.

The regression analysis aims to see if there are systematic patterns between the turning points in the recession variables—the variables that reflect the current state of the economy—and the turning points (or the period of first tightening) of the policy variables. To do this, we estimate an equation like that presented in (1).

$$tp\_policy_i = \beta_0 + \beta_1 tp\_recession_i + \varepsilon_i. \tag{1}$$

In (1), the variable tp_policy consists of the turning (tightening) points for a policy variable of interest, such as the federal funds rate, for each recession in our sample. The explanatory variable $tp\_recession$ consists of the turning point of a recession variable. For both variables, the tightening and turning points are measured in the number of quarters after the official NBER trough date for that cycle.

If the recession variable does not influence the Federal Reserve's decision to tighten monetary policy, then we would not expect a relationship between the turning point of the recession variable and the turning point of the policy variable. In this case, we would expect an estimate of β_1 that was close to 0 and insignificant. If the Federal Reserve always waited for the recession variable to turn before tightening, then we would expect an estimate of β_1 that was positive and significant. An estimate of β_1 close to 1 would suggest that the Federal Reserve always tightened on or about the same quarter in which the recession variable turned. An estimate of β_1 much larger than 1 would suggest that the Federal Reserve always waited until after the recession variable had turned before it tightened the policy variable, and an estimate of β_1 that was positive and less than 1 would suggest that the Federal Reserve would be influenced by the turning point of the recession variable, but would not always wait for that variable to turn before tightening the policy variable.

Obviously there may be more than one recession variable that the Federal Reserve watches, but given our small sample size, we are not able to estimate a fully specified model. Instead we estimate a number of versions of (1) with each policy variable regressed on each recession variable. Only if a recession variable is significant and positive for a majority of the policy variables do we suggest there is evidence of a systematic relationship between the recession variable and the Federal Reserve's decision to tighten.

TABLE 8-3

ESTIMATES FOR SLOPE COEFFICIENT IN EQUATION (1)

(POST–WORLD WAR II SAMPLE)

Explanatory Variables	Policy Variables						
	Narra-tives	Federal Funds	Real Federal Funds	Base Growth	Real Base Growth	M2 Growth	Real M2 Growth
Inflation (GNP)	1.480	1.240	−0.710	0.730	1.000	−0.190	0.080
	(0.610)	(0.400)	(0.340)	(0.270)	(0.120)	(0.200)	(0.120)
	[0.04]	[0.02]	[0.07]	[0.03]	[0.00]	[0.36]	[0.53]
Inflation (CPI)	1.200	1.000	−0.810	1.000	0.930	−0.500	0.190
	(1.210)	(1.290)	(1.770)	(0.390)	(0.720)	(0.500)	(0.310)
	[0.35]	[0.47]	[0.66]	[0.03]	[0.23]	[0.34]	[0.56]
Real GNP	−2.060	−0.330	−0.710	−1.100	−1.210	−0.260	0.620
	(2.590)	(1.610)	(1.650)	(0.980)	(1.220)	(0.820)	(0.460)
	[0.45]	[0.84]	[0.68]	[0.30]	[0.35]	[0.76]	[0.22]
Ind. Prod.	2.180	3.510	−0.100	1.000	0.890	0.200	0.280
	(1.980)	(2.570)	(1.590)	(0.470)	(1.040)	(0.630)	(0.360)
	[0.30]	[0.21]	[0.95]	[0.07]	[0.42]	[0.75]	[0.46]
Output Gap	2.190	2.100	1.370	0.350	0.340	0.480	−0.120
	(0.690)	(0.340)	(0.430)	(0.510)	(0.480)	(0.230)	(0.160)
	[0.01]	[0.00]	[0.02]	[0.51]	[0.50]	[0.07]	[0.47]
Unemployment	1.440	1.430	0.710	0.530	0.320	0.480	0.010
	(0.330)	(0.120)	(0.160)	(0.250)	(0.280)	(0.100)	(0.100)
	[0.00]	[0.00]	[0.00]	[0.07]	[0.30]	[0.00]	[0.91]

SOURCE: Authors' calculations.

Tables 7-3 and 7-4 report the estimates of β_1 for each regression for each sample. Table 7-3 reports the estimates of β_1 from (1) for the post–World War II sample. Table 7-4 reports the estimates of β_1 from (1) for the whole sample excluding the two cycles around World War II.[4]

Because of the small samples (ten observations for the post–World War II sample and fourteen for the whole sample), the least squares estimates of (1) are likely to be highly sensitive to outliers and influential observations. To mitigate this problem, a robust estimator was used to estimate (1). The robust estimator used was an iteratively reweighted least squares procedure found in Holland and Welsch (1977).[5] This estimator is robust to those observations whose ordinary least squares (OLS) residuals are large.

TABLE 8-4

ESTIMATES FOR SLOPE COEFFICIENT IN EQUATION (1) (FULL SAMPLE)

Explanatory Variables	Policy Variables						
	Narra-tives	Policy Rate[a]	Real Policy Rate	Base Growth	Real Base Growth	M2 Growth	Real M2 Growth
Price Level /Inflation[b] (GNP)	0.100 (0.40) [0.81]	0.840 (0.33) [0.03]	1.120 (0.45) [0.03]	0.660 (0.26) [0.03]	0.560 (0.25) [0.04]	−0.020 (0.20) [0.93]	0.150 (0.20) [0.45]
Price Level /Inflation (CPI)	−0.560 (1.02) [0.59]	0.630 (0.62) [0.33]	−0.160 (1.04) [0.88]	0.580 (0.57) [0.33]	−0.120 (0.54) [0.83]	0.460 (0.30) [0.15]	0.120 (0.37) [0.74]
Real GNP	−0.940 (1.22) [0.46]	−0.480 (1.03) [0.65]	1.990 (2.46) [0.44]	−1.070 (0.94) [0.28]	−0.240 (0.89) [0.79]	−0.850 (0.63) [0.20]	0.280 (0.62) [0.66]
Ind. Prod.	1.020 (1.22) [0.42]	−0.370 (0.81) [0.65]	−0.500 (1.37) [0.72]	−0.340 (0.72) [0.65]	−0.180 (0.65) [0.79]	0.250 (0.45) [0.59]	−0.710 (0.43) [0.12]
Output Gap	1.480 (0.54) [0.02]	1.930 (0.40) [0.00]	4.170 (0.50) [0.00]	−0.140 (0.41) [0.74]	0.090 (0.38) [0.82]	−0.750 (0.19) [0.00]	−0.300 (0.23) [0.21]
Unemployment	1.030 (0.34) [0.01]	0.990 (0.29) [0.01]	0.690 (0.32) [0.06]	−0.070 (0.21) [0.76]	−0.100 (0.19) [0.62]	0.450 (0.07) [0.00]	−0.270 (0.12) [0.05]

SOURCE: Authors' calculations.

[a] The policy rate is the federal funds rate after 1954 and the discount rate before 1954.

[b] For cycles up to and including the one ending in 1957Q2, the turning point used is for the price level. For recessions after 1957Q2, the turning point for inflation is used.

As discussed above, we do not have enough observations to estimate a fully specified version of (1). The second approach we take is to estimate (1) for different policy variables in a system. The utility of the system estimator is to increase the effective sample size, which will allow the inclusion of more than one recession variable in the estimation of (1). To get the increase in effective sample size, we impose equality constraints on the slope coefficients while allowing the constants to differ across equations. We also take into account any correlation between the errors of the equations by estimating the system using a one-step feasible generalized least squares (GLS) estimator. The system estimated is:

$$y_{1i} = \beta_{10} + \beta_1 x_{1i} + \ldots + \beta_{ki} x_{ki} + \varepsilon_{1i}$$
$$\vdots \qquad\qquad\qquad\qquad , \qquad\qquad (2)$$
$$y_{ni} = \beta_{n0} + \beta_1 x_{1i} + \ldots + \beta_{ki} x_{ki} + \varepsilon_{ni}$$

where $E(\varepsilon\varepsilon') = \begin{bmatrix} \sigma_1^2 & \cdots & \sigma_{1n} \\ \vdots & \ddots & \vdots \\ \sigma_{n1} & \cdots & \sigma_n^2 \end{bmatrix}$ and $\sigma_{ij} \neq 0$ for all i and j. In (2) the variable y_i

is the tightening point of policy variable i, and the variable x_i is the turning point of the recession variable j.

The systems estimates are reported for post–World War II samples and for the whole sample in tables 8-5 and 8-6. The systems are chosen so the dependent variables are similar in nature. Thus, nominal policy variables such as the growth rate of the nominal money base would be included with the growth rate of nominal M2 and the nominal policy interest rate (the federal funds rate after 1954 and the nominal discount rate before 1954). Real variables will be included with other real variables.

We must emphasize that the aim of this exercise is not to identify any causal relationships between any of the recession variables and the decision to tighten; rather we aim to find evidence of any systematic relationship between when the Federal Reserve tightened and when some or all of the recession variables turned. Our hope is that this exercise will sharpen our analysis and give us the ability to predict when the Federal Reserve will start to tighten during the current business cycle.

Lessons from the Individual Regressions

The Post–World War II Period. Table 8-3 reports the results for the estimation of equation (1) using a robust estimator. The point estimates, the standard errors (in round brackets), and the p-values (in square brackets) are reported for all the combinations of policy and recession variables used in our analysis.[6] The slope coefficients reported in tables 8-3 and 8-4 can be interpreted as the expected change in the time it takes for the Fed to tighten the particular dependent variable, given a one-quarter increase in the turning point of the explanatory variable from the NBER recession trough. The

TABLE 8-5
ESTIMATES FOR SLOPE COEFFICIENT IN EQUATION (2)
(POST–WORLD WAR II)

Variable	{Narr, FFR}		{FFR, Base}		{Real FFR, Real Base}	
Inflation (GNP)	0.89	0.60	0.71	0.51	0.87	0.74
	(0.1)	(0.1)	(0.1)	(0.0)	(0.1)	(0.1)
	[0.0]	[0.0]	[0.0]	[0.0]	[0.0]	[0.0]
Output Gap	1.85	0.76	0.99	–0.18	0.58	–0.65
	(0.1)	(0.3)	(0.1)	(0.4)	(0.1)	(0.6)
	[0.0]	[0.05]	[0.00]	[0.70]	[0.00]	[0.32]
Unemployment		1.20	0.94	0.72	0.97	0.46	1.03
	(0.14)	(0.22)	(0.08)	(0.30)	(0.12)	(0.41)
	[0.00]	[0.00]	[0.00]	[0.00]	[0.00]	[0.02]

SOURCE: Authors' calculations.

results suggest that three variables—GNP inflation, the output gap, and unemployment—appear to affect the decision to tighten.

Unemployment appears to delay the date at which the Fed tightens when we use the dates extracted from the narratives, the main policy rate (the federal funds rate), the real policy rate, and the rate of growth of the money base. The coefficients on unemployment are all positive, suggesting that the longer it takes for unemployment to start declining, the longer it takes the Fed to tighten.

The other macroeconomic aggregate that consistently affects policy variables is the output gap. The slope coefficient of equation (1), when output gap is used as the explanatory variable, is significant and positive for the turning points identified from the narratives, the policy rate, and the real policy rate. Unlike unemployment, however, the output gap does not significantly affect money base growth. Both the output gap and unemployment also positively affect M2 growth.

The other real macroeconomic aggregates, real GNP and industrial production, do not affect the policy variables except that industrial production does have a significant effect on the rate of growth of the money base. Thus, it appears that the only real variables that consistently affect a majority of the policy variables are unemployment and the output gap.

TABLE 8-6
ESTIMATES FOR SLOPE COEFFICIENT IN EQUATION (2) (FULL SAMPLE)

Variable	{Narr, Policy Rate}		{Policy Rate, Base}		{Real Policy Rate, Real Base}	
Price Level/	0.90	0.85	0.78	0.76	0.85	0.95
Inflation (GNP)	(0.46)	(0.54)	(0.26)	(0.23)	(0.25)	(0.25)
	[0.06]	[0.13]	[0.00]	[0.00]	[0.00]	[0.00]
Output Gap	1.48	2.80	0.61	1.14	0.33	1.46
	(0.59)	(0.99)	(0.34)	(0.70)	(0.33)	(0.64)
	[0.02]	[0.01]	[0.08]	[0.11]	[0.32]	[0.03]
Unemployment	0.22	−0.90	0.06	−0.37	−0.16	−0.58
	(0.37)	(0.62)	(0.15)	(0.37)	(0.16)	(0.31)
	[0.56]	[0.13]	[0.68]	[0.32]	[0.32]	[0.08]

SOURCE: Authors' calculations.

We also looked at the effect the price level and inflation had on the decision to tighten. From table 8-3 we see that inflation constructed from the GNP deflator has a significant and positive effect on all the policy variables except for M2 growth and real M2 growth. GNP inflation is the only variable that significantly affects growth of the real money base. While inflation is significant, it presents troubling results. The slope coefficient for inflation when the real federal funds rate is used as the dependent variable in equation (1) is negative. Further inspection of the data used to estimate equation (1) shows that there is one observation that is treated by the robust estimator as an outlier. Unfortunately, this observation, while statistically an outlier, is actually a useful piece of information. The observation taken during the recession from 1990Q3 to 2000Q4 causes this problem. In this recession, inflation turned five quarters after the NBER trough date, and the real federal funds rate turned eight quarters after the NBER trough date. This observation falls in line with our previous belief that the Fed would wait to tighten after it observes inflation starting to increase. Taking this observation out of the regression leads to a negative coefficient, while leaving it in and giving it equal weight (that is, using OLS) gives us a positive and significant coefficient. This suggests that the negative coefficient we have estimated is more a function of our statistical procedure and the fact that we have small samples than an actual relationship.

Thus, from the post–World War II sample, there appears to be a systematic, positive relationship between the length of time it takes for inflation to increase, for the output gap to increase, or for the unemployment rate to decrease and the length of time the Fed waits to tighten. However, it is difficult to draw any inferences from the actual size of the coefficients as reported, as our sample sizes are small. We are not able to include these variables in a regression equation at the same time. Clearly the estimates are going to suffer from omitted variable bias, so at present we do not know which variables are more important than others. We attempt to find a solution for this problem by using the system estimator given in equation (2). Before reporting the system estimates for the post–World War II period, we first need to check if the relationship we found extends back to the interwar period.

Full Sample. Table 8-4 reports the estimates of the slope coefficients for equation (1) using the larger sample that includes the business cycles from the interwar period. There is a problem in that the main policy rate used after World War II—the federal funds rate—did not exist before 1954. Before 1954, the Fed used the discount rate. However, the discount rate did not change much during the 1930s and was not the main instrument for monetary policy then. To estimate a model for the whole period, we needed to construct a number of composite variables.

The first variable constructed was a composite policy rate variable. This variable was made up of the turning points for the federal funds rate after 1954 and the turning points for the discount rate before 1954. However, after the recession of 1929Q3–1937Q1, the discount rate became ineffective in the face of expected deflation and was not changed after 1933. For that period, we used the turning point from the narratives. The second composite variable that we constructed was the composite price level/inflation variable. This reflects the fact that, before the 1960s, inflation in the United States was not persistent and the Fed was primarily concerned with monitoring the price level. It was only after the recession ending in 1957Q2 that inflation became important. Thus, the composite price level/inflation variable consists of turning points for the price level up to the recession ending in 1957Q2, and thereafter consists of the turning points of inflation.

The results are strikingly similar to the results we obtained for the post–World War II period. The output gap and the unemployment rate are significant and positive for the whole period, and the only change is that now these two variables no longer significantly affect the growth of the money base. The composite price level/inflation variable significantly and positively affects the policy rate, the real policy rate, the growth of the money base, and the growth of the real money base. It is interesting to note that when the sample is slightly increased, the effect of the price level/inflation rate is no longer negative on the real policy rate. This further strengthens our contention that the inflation rate also has a positive and significant effect on the real policy rate in the post–World War II period.

The conclusion of all these individual regressions is that there is a significant and positive relationship between the output gap, unemployment, and the price level/inflation rate and the length of time it takes for the Fed to tighten after a recession. As noted earlier, however, the sample size and the fact that all these results are from simple linear regressions did not allow us to judge the relative importance of each variable. In the next section, we report system estimates that allowed us to include more than one variable at a time in our regression. We also must note that the output gap variable and the unemployment rate variable are highly correlated, so the results we obtained in table 8-3 for either variable may be picking up the same effect. The only way we can check which variable is important is to include them both in the same regression. We do that using the system estimator described in (2).

Lessons from the System Regressions

Tables 8-5 and 8-6 report the results for equation (2), where a system of seemingly unrelated equations is estimated. The tables report results for a number of different systems: the turning points from the narratives, the turning points from the federal funds rate, the nominal variables (the federal funds rate and the rate of growth of the money base), and the real variables (the real federal funds rate and the rate of growth of the real money base).

Post–World War II Sample. For each system, three separate equations are estimated: one with inflation and the output gap, one with inflation and unemployment, and one with the output gap and unemployment. The first thing to notice from table 8-5 is that the estimate on inflation ranges from 0.51 to 0.89 with the median value of 0.73. The estimates on the other variable in the equation with inflation included are significant and significantly higher than the estimates for inflation for the systems based on the nominal variables, suggesting that more emphasis is placed on the real side of the economy in the post–World War II period when setting the nominal variables. Given that the output gap and unemployment are highly correlated (a correlation of 0.88 in the postwar sample), it is uncertain whether these variables are picking up the same information. To find out, a third regression is run with both unemployment and output gap included. We see that unemployment is always significant in these regressions, with output gap only significant in the system with the turning point constructed from the narratives and the federal funds rate. Even in this system, the coefficient on the output gap is smaller than unemployment. These results together suggest that unemployment and inflation were the important variables that the Fed watched in the postwar period.

The Full Sample. Table 8-6 contains the results for the full sample using the composite variables used in the individual analysis. The results for the output gap and unemployment in the full sample are not as robust as in the post–World War II sample. One striking result is that, for the full sample, the coefficients on the price level/inflation variable are now higher than in the postwar sample. The estimates range from 0.76 to 0.95 with a median estimate of 0.85. This suggests that if we had enough data to estimate the interwar period separately from the postwar period, the coefficient on price level/inflation would be higher than in the postwar period. A tentative conclusion is that the Fed was more sensitive to the aggregate price level during the interwar period than in the postwar period.

However, the results for the output gap and the unemployment rate are not as consistent as in the postwar period. Again, a tentative conclusion is that the Fed has emphasized the real side of the economy more after World War II than it did before or during the interwar period. There is evidence that the Fed did take into account the real side before World War II, but that it was the output gap and not the unemployment rate that was important.

Thus, our results suggest that the real side played a more significant role after World War II. Our results also indicate that inflation (or price level before the war) is important for both periods, with some evidence suggesting that there is less emphasis on prices after World War II than during the interwar period.

Predictions for the Most Recent Recession

Given our estimates for (1) and (2), we are now interested in predicting, based on current data, the dates of tightening for each of the important policy variables. The policy variables we make predictions for are the tightening date based on the historical narratives, the tightening date for the federal funds rate, the tightening date for the real federal funds rate, the tightening date for the growth rate of the money base, and the tightening date for the rate of growth of the real money base. Table 8-7 contains the predictions

TABLE 8-7
PREDICTED TIGHTENING DATES (QUARTERS AFTER 2009Q2)

Variable	Narratives	Federal Funds Rate	Real Federal Funds Rate	Base Growth	Real Base Growth
Inflation (GNP)	4.52	2.94	−0.44	1.37	1.00
Output Gap	1.78	1.02	0.41	0.38	0.27
Unemployment	3.65	2.99	1.25	0.35	0.43
{Inf, Out Gap}	3.22	2.23			
{Inf, Unemp.}	4.24	3.24			
{Out Gap, Unemp.}	3.08	2.08			
{Inf, Out Gap}		2.71		0.60	
{Inf, Unemp.}		3.21		1.10	
{Out Gap, Unemp.}		2.81		0.70	
{Inf, Out Gap}			2.31		0.98
{Inf, Unemp.}			2.58		1.25
{Out Gap, Unemp.}			2.28		0.95

SOURCE: Authors' calculations.

NOTES: These predictions are based on predicted turning points for inflation, the output gap, and unemployment of 1, 0, and 2 respectively.

based on our estimate of the tightening dates using inflation, output gap, and unemployment as our predictors. The National Bureau of Economic Research has determined that the most recent recession ended in June of 2009, so we use 2009Q2 as the trough date of the current business cycle.

To predict the tightening dates, we need predictions of the turning points for these three predictor series. Figures 8-2 through 8-4 show the values of these three variables for the most recent cycle. Figure 8-2 reports the value for the inflation rate based on the GNP deflator. It is quite clear from this figure that inflation, measured using the GNP deflator, turned during the third quarter of 2009. Thus, we will use 2009Q3 as the turning point for inflation. We label this one quarter after the trough date. Figure 8-3 shows the output gap measured as the percentage deviation from the Hodrick-Prescott filter trend of log real output. It appears that the output gap turned in the second quarter of 2009, so we use 0 as the turning point

FIGURE 8-2
INFLATION RATE FOR 2007–2011

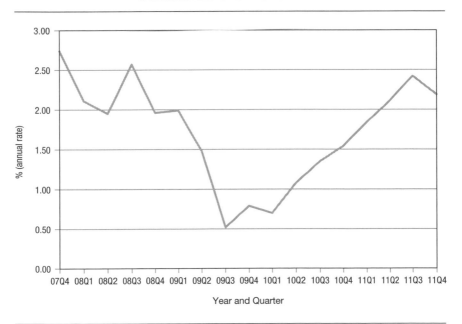

SOURCE: Federal Reserve Economic Database.

FIGURE 8-3
OUTPUT GAP FOR 2007–2011

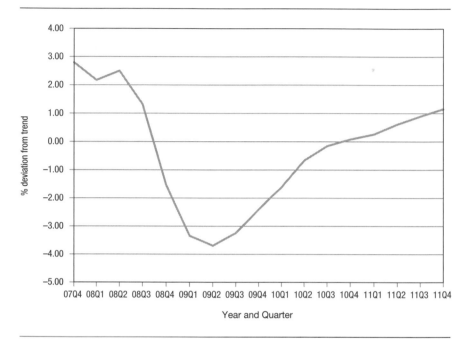

SOURCE: Federal Reserve Economic Database.

for the output gap (measured relative to the business cycle trough date). Figure 8-4 shows the unemployment rate for the most recent cycle. Unemployment appears to have peaked in the fourth quarter of 2009, although the decline from the peak appears to be slow. For unemployment we use figure 8-2 for our prediction. Unemployment is the only variable of the three that we follow for which the recovery after the turning point is not sharp. Thus there may be some doubt as to whether unemployment has indeed turned or instead has plateaued. This may lead to some policy uncertainty if, as we showed above, policymakers have put more emphasis on unemployment in the more recent exits.

These turning points were used to generate the predicted tightening dates for the various policy variables. The predicted tightening dates for the federal funds rate using the individual regressions reflect the differences in turning points in the predictors. Using inflation or unemployment, we

FIGURE 8-4
UNEMPLOYMENT RATE FOR 2007–2011

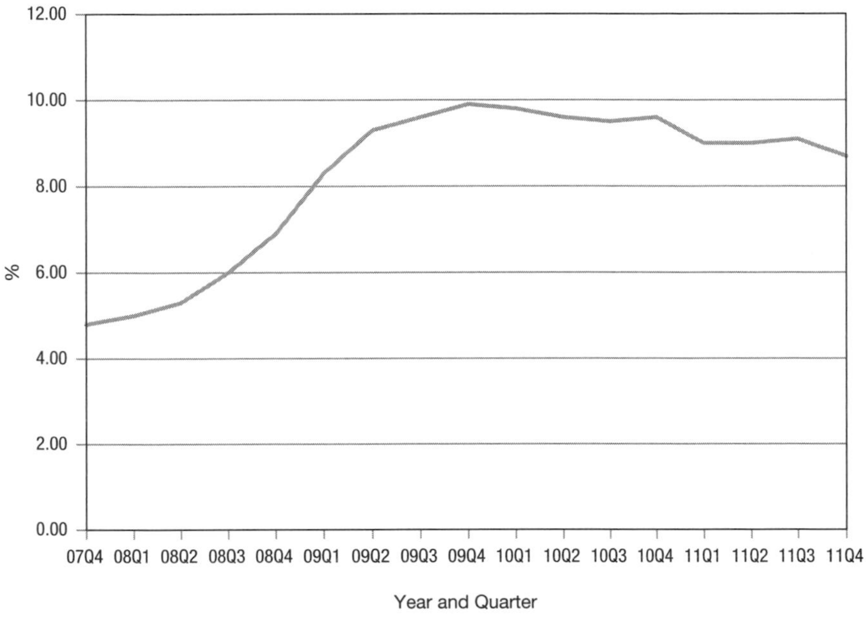

Year and Quarter

SOURCE: Federal Reserve Economic Database.

get predicted tightening dates for the nominal federal funds rate or the narrative rate between three and four and a half quarters after the trough date, suggesting Fed tightening sometime in late 2010. Using the systems estimates, a similar and consistent picture emerges. The predicted tightening dates for these models range from two quarters after the trough date to just over four quarters after the trough date. The predicted tightening dates for the growth of the monetary base and real monetary base are slightly earlier, with tightening predicted to occur approximately two quarters after the trough date (2009Q2). This reflects the observation that the monetary base has typically tightened earlier than the nominal policy rates over the post–World War II sample.

Obviously our predictions, which are based on past observations, have not turned out to be accurate. As of May 2012, the Fed has not officially tightened. One reason for this might be that unemployment has not declined enough for the Fed to be comfortable enough to start tightening. The experience of the previous two exits suggests that the Fed has waited for unemployment to fall before moving to tighten. Another reason could be that the optimum value of the federal funds rate is negative so that we cannot observe a tightening of this variable yet; we have to wait for the optimal federal funds rate to become positive before we will see evidence of tightening. In fact, the nonstandard monetary policy that the Fed has pursued since 2007 can be viewed as being equivalent to cutting the federal funds rate. The lack of a third round of quantitative easing and the rolling back of positions may, as some Fed officials have argued, constitute a tightening of the implicit federal funds rate. In time we may look back at the narratives of this period and see that tightening may already have begun, just that tightening did not manifest itself as an increase in the federal funds rate.

Conclusion

This chapter presents historical narrative, descriptive, and econometric evidence on the timing of monetary policy in the United States over fourteen business cycles from 1920 to 2007. We evaluate the monetary exits with respect to the turning points of principal macro-aggregates (especially unemployment and inflation).

In general, we found that monetary policy tightens close to when unemployment peaks and when inflation troughs, but that the timing is usually dominated by unemployment. We also find that, on a number of occasions, monetary policy measured by the monetary base (real and nominal) shows a different pattern than the official policy interest rates.

We found that the timing evidence differed between the interwar period (and in some ways the 1950s) and the postwar period in a number of respects: First, inflation was not persistent in the interwar period (or until the 1960s), so the measure of price stability that mattered most was the price level. In the 1920s and 1950s, policy tightened when the price level began to rise. Second, in the 1920s and 1950s, tightening occurred when prices rose and before unemployment peaked. We found a few episodes where tightening occurred before recessions ended, suggesting that the Fed was following countercyclical policy.

Beginning in the mid-1960s, inflation increased and became persistent for close to twenty years. In those cycles, the timing of the tightening does not show that the pace of tightening was not sufficient to reduce the rising trend in inflation. Although inflation was reduced significantly beginning with the Great Moderation, the timing of policy tightening still favored unemployment.

There are several possible reasons for these patterns: First, in the interwar period, the Fed followed gold-standard orthodoxy, which placed primary importance on price stability. Second, after World War II and the Employment Act of 1945, the Fed followed a dual mandate for price stability and high employment. Third, beginning in the 1960s, the Fed adhered to Keynesian theories and the Phillips Curve, which attached primary importance to low unemployment over low inflation. Fourth, the dominance of unemployment in the timing of tightening in the postwar era reflects, in addition to the influence of Keynesian theory, political pressure by Congress and the administration not to tighten while unemployment was unacceptably high. Fifth, even in the Great Moderation, when inflation had been significantly reduced and considerable emphasis had been placed on the importance of a credible nominal anchor, the timing of exits favored unemployment. This was evident in the last two cycles. In both cases of jobless recoveries, political pressure may have been important.

How will the exit strategy play out for the current cycle? The evidence suggests that were the timing patterns of the postwar era followed in the current cycle, with unemployment peaking in the fourth quarter of 2009, then we should have seen a tightening in the first half of 2010. This did not happen, and there is little evidence that policy will change any time soon. The experience since 2010 is consistent with the view that the Fed has attached top priority to the unemployment part of the dual mandate. It has felt justified in doing so because measures of the core inflation rate have been below their 2 percent implicit target rate. It also may be responding to political pressure to fight unemployment. If, as some have argued, incipient inflationary pressure observant in global commodity markets and reflecting past monetary expansion leads to a run-up in headline inflation and in inflationary expectations, then the Fed will have waited too late to tighten. Only the future will tell if its current strategy is correct.

References

Balke, Nathan S., and Robert J. Gordon. 1986. "Historical Data (Appendix B)." Vol. 25 of *The American Business Cycle: Continuity and Change*, edited by Robert J. Gordon. Chicago: University of Chicago Press.

Bernanke, Ben S., and Cara S. Lown. 1991. "The Credit Crunch." *Brookings Papers on Economic Activity*, no. 2: 205–247.

Bordo, Michael, and Barry Eichengreen. 2008. "Bretton Woods and the Great Inflation." NBER Working Paper 14532.

Bordo, Michael, Christopher Erceg, Andrew Levin, and Ryan Michaels. 2007. "Three Great American Disinflations." NBER Working Paper 12982.

Bordo, Michael, and Joseph Haubrich. 2009. "Credit Crises, Money, and Contractions: An Historical View." NBER Working Paper 15389.

———. 2012. "Deep Recessions, Fast Recoveries, and Financial Crises: Evidence from the American Record." Rutgers University (mimeo). May.

Claessens, Stijn, M. Ayhan Kose, and Marco Terrones. 2008. "What Happens during Recessions, Crunches, and Busts?" IMF Working Paper 08/274.

Cole, Hal, and Lee Ohanian. 2004. "New Deal Policies and the Persistence of the Great Depression: A General Equilibrium Analysis." *Journal of Political Economy* 112(4): 779–816.

Eggertsson, Gautti. 2008. "Great Expectations and the End of the Depression." *American Economic Review* 94(4): 1476–1516.

Friedman, Milton. 1953. "The Effects of a Full Employment Policy on Economic Stability: A Formal Analysis." In *Essays in Positive Economics*. Chicago: University of Chicago Press.

Friedman, Milton, and Anna J. Schwartz. 1963. *A Monetary History of the United States: 1867 to 1960*. Princeton: Princeton University Press.

Hetzel, Robert. 2008. *The Monetary Policy of the Federal Reserve: A History*. New York: Cambridge University Press.

Holland, Paul W., and Roy E. Welsch. 1977. "Robust Regression Using Iteratively Reweighted Least-Squares." *Communications in Statistics: Theory and Methods*, A6, 813–827.

International Monetary Fund. 2008. *World Economic Outlook*.

Meltzer, Allan H. 2003. *A History of the Federal Reserve, Volume I: 1913–1951*. Chicago: University of Chicago Press.

———. 2010. *A History of the Federal Reserve, Volume II: 1951–1987*. Chicago: University of Chicago Press.

Mussa, Michael. 2009. "Global Economic Prospects as of September 2009: Onward to Global Recovery." Washington, DC: Peterson Institute. September.

Reinhart, Carmen, and Kenneth S. Rogoff. 2009. *This Time Is Different: Eight Centuries of Financial Folly*. Princeton: Princeton University Press.

Romer, Christina. 1992. "What Ended the Great Depression?" *Journal of Economic History* 52 (December): 757–784.

Romer, Christina, and David Romer. 1994. "Monetary Policy Matters." *Journal of Monetary Economics* 34 (August): 75–88.

Stock, James, and Mark Watson. 2012. " Disentangling the Channels of the 2007–2009 Recession." NBER Working Paper 18094. May.

Notes

1. Friedman (1953) was the first to analyze the difficulty of achieving the pace and timing for successful countercyclical policy.

2. The Fed did not have GNP or unemployment data during the interwar period (these data were constructed after World War II). Moreover, it did not think about recessions in terms of output gaps. It did, however, have data on industrial production. Nevertheless, we use the available modern data on GNP and unemployment to make comparisons between the post–World War II era and the interwar period.

3. By recession variables, we mean those variables that depict the turning point of the recession to expansions. These variables are the real variables (output, industrial production, unemployment, output gap) and the price/inflation variables.

4. The omitted cycles are 1937Q2–1944Q4 and 1945Q1–1948Q3.

5. The weight function used in the iteratively reweighted least squares procedure was the "biweight" weight function. The *robustfit* command of Matlab's Statistics Toolbox was used to implement the robust estimation procedure used in this chapter.

6. We also looked at financial variables such as the term spread, the quality spread, and the return to the S&P500 but did not find any systematic relationship between the policy variable turning points and the financial variables. We do not report these results here, for the sake of brevity. These results are available from the authors upon request.

Chapter Appendix

TABLE 8-A1
DATA DEFINITIONS

Variable	Source
Discount Rate	Obtained from the Board of Governors database (H.15). Before 1954, the discount rate is the Federal Reserve Bank of New York discount rate. The discount rate series is discontinued after 2002, and the discount window primary credit rate is used after 2002. Monthly data converted to quarterly data using quarterly averages.
Federal Funds Rate	Effective federal funds rate (FEDFUNDS): Obtained from Federal Reserve Bank of St. Louis database (FRED).[a] Monthly data converted to quarterly data using quarterly averages. Real rate obtained by subtracting inflation rate (computed using GNP deflator).
Money Base	St. Louis Adjusted Monetary Base (AMBSL seasonally adjusted): obtained from FRED. Monthly data converted to quarterly data using quarterly averages. Real rate obtained by dividing by GNP deflator. Growth rates are one-quarter growth rates expressed as an annualized rate.
M2	M2 from Balke and Gordon (1986) until 1983. After 1983 used M2 series from FRED database (seasonally adjusted, M2SL). Monthly data converted to quarterly data using quarterly averages. The two series were spliced at join. Real data obtained by dividing by GNP deflator. Growth rates are one-quarter growth rates expressed as an annualized rate.
Price Level (GNP)	GNP deflator obtained from Balke and Gordon (1986) until 1983. After that, used GNP deflator from FRED database (seasonally adjusted, GNPDEF). The two series were spliced at join.
Price Level (CPI)	Consumer price index for all urban consumers: all items. Obtained from FRED database (CPIAUCNS). Monthly data converted to quarterly data using quarterly averages.

Variable	Source
Inflation (GNP)	Percentage one-quarter change in GNP deflator expressed at an annualized rate.
Inflation (CPI)	Percentage one-quarter change in CPI expressed at an annualized rate.
Real GNP	Real gross national product obtained from Balke and Gordon (1986) for periods until 1983. After that, used quarterly GNP data from FRED database (GNP). GNP price deflator from FRED spliced with Balke and Gordon (1986) price deflator. Real GNP after 1983 is nominal GNP divided by spliced GNP deflator series.
Industrial Production	Obtained from FRED database (INDPRO). Monthly series converted to quarterly series using quarterly averages.
Unemployment	Obtained from Bureau of Labor Statistics. Unemployment rate: civilian labor force (LNS14000000, seasonally adjusted). Monthly data converted to quarterly data using quarterly averages.
Output Gap	Proportional deviation of real GNP from long-run trend. Computed as the deviations of the logarithm of real GNP from its long-run trend as computed using Hodrick-Prescott filter with smoothing parameter $\lambda = 1600$.

[a] http://research.stlouisfed.org/fred2/

TABLE 8-A2a

TURNING DATES: POLICY VARIABLES, 1920–1937

Cycle	Narra-tives	Discount Rate	Real Discount Rate	Base Growth	Real Base Growth	M2 Growth	Real M2 Growth
1. 20Q1–23Q1 (1921Q3)[a]	1922Q2	1922Q4	—	1922Q4	1921Q4	1922Q1	1922Q1
2. 23Q2–26Q2 (1924Q3)	1925Q2	1924Q4	1925Q1	1924Q3	1925Q1	1924Q2	1925Q1
3. 26Q3–29Q2 (1927Q4)	1928Q1	1927Q4	1927Q4	1928Q1	1927Q4	1927Q4	1927Q4
4. 29Q3–37Q1 (1933Q1)	1936Q3	—	—	1933Q4	1933Q4	1932Q3	1934Q1

[a] Dates in parentheses are the NBER trough dates for each cycle. Missing values represent a cycle in which no definitive turning point was identified.

TABLE 8-A2b

TURNING DATES: MACRO AGGREGATES, 1920–1937

Cycle	Price Level (GNP Deflator)	Price Level (CPI)	Real GNP	Industrial Production	Output Gap	Unemploy-ment
1. 20Q1–23Q1 (1921Q3)[a]	1922Q2	1922Q1	1921Q1	1921Q1	1921Q1	1921Q1
2. 23Q2–26Q2 (1924Q3)	1924Q3	1924Q1	1924Q3	1924Q2	1924Q3	1924Q1
3. 26Q3–29Q2 (1927Q4)	1927Q2	1928Q1	1927Q4	1927Q4	1927Q4	1928Q1
4. 29Q3–37Q1 (1933Q1)	1933Q1	1933Q1	1933Q1	1933Q1	1933Q1	1932Q1

[a] Dates in parentheses are the NBER trough dates for each cycle.

TABLE 8-A3a

TURNING DATES: POLICY VARIABLES, 1948–2007

Cycle	Narratives	Federal Funds Rate (Discount Rate)	Real Federal Funds Rate (Real Discount Rate)	Base Growth	Real Base Growth	M2 Growth	Real M2 Growth
1. 48Q4–53Q1 (1949Q4)[a]	1949Q2	(1950Q2)	(1951Q1)	1949Q2	1949Q2	1950Q1	1949Q4
2. 53Q2–57Q2 (1954Q2)	1955Q1	1954Q4	1954Q3	1954Q3	1954Q3	1954Q2	1954Q2
3. 57Q3–60Q1 (1958Q2)	1958Q3	1958Q2	1958Q2	1958Q1	1958Q1	1958Q1	1958Q1
4. 60Q2–69Q3 (1961Q1)	1961Q2	1961Q2	1961Q3	1961Q3	1961Q3	1961Q1	1960Q4
5. 69Q4–73Q3 (1970Q4)	1971Q1	1971Q1	1971Q1	1970Q4	1970Q2	1971Q1	1971Q1
6. 73Q4–79Q4 (1975Q1)	1975Q1	1975Q2	1975Q1	1975Q1	1975Q1	1975Q1	1975Q1
7. 80Q1–81Q2 (1980Q3)	1981Q2	1980Q3	1980Q3	1980Q2	1980Q2	1980Q2	1980Q2
8. 81Q3–90Q2 (1982Q4)	1983Q3	1983Q1	1982Q3	1982Q4	1983Q1	1982Q4	1982Q4
9. 90Q3–00Q4 (1991Q1)	1994Q1	1993Q2	1993Q2	1992Q2	1992Q2	1990Q4	1991Q1
10. 01Q1–07Q3 (2001Q4)	2004Q2	2004Q2	2003Q1	2001Q4	2001Q4	2002Q3	2001Q3

[a] Dates in parentheses are the NBER trough dates for each cycle.

TABLE 8-A3b

TURNING DATES: MACRO AGGREGATES, 1948–2007

Cycle	Inflation (GNP) (Price Level)	Inflation (CPI) (Price Level)	Real GNP	Industrial Production	Output Gap	Unemployment
1. 48Q4–53Q1 (1949Q4)[a]	1949Q4 (1950Q1)	1949Q2 (1950Q1)	1949Q4	1949Q2	1949Q4	1949Q4
2. 53Q2–57Q2 (1954Q2)	1954Q2 (1953Q4)	1954Q3 (1954Q4)	1954Q1	1954Q1	1954Q2	1954Q3
3. 57Q3–60Q1 (1958Q2)	1958Q1	1958Q2	1958Q1	1958Q1	1958Q2	1958Q2
4. 60Q2–69Q3 (1961Q1)	1960Q4	1961Q1	1960Q4	1960Q4	1961Q1	1961Q2
5. 69Q4–73Q3 (1970Q4)	1970Q2	1970Q4	1970Q4	1970Q4	1970Q4	1971Q3
6. 73Q4–79Q4 (1975Q1)	1975Q1	1975Q1	1975Q1	1975Q1	1975Q1	1975Q2
7. 80Q1–81Q2 (1980Q3)	1980Q2	1980Q2	1980Q3	1980Q2	1980Q3	1980Q3
8. 81Q3–90Q2 (1982Q4)	1983Q1	1982Q4	1982Q3	1982Q4	1982Q4	1982Q4
9. 90Q3–00Q4 (1991Q1)	1984Q1	1991Q1	1991Q1	1991Q1	1991Q3	1984Q2
10. 01Q1–07Q3 (2001Q4)	2001Q3	2001Q3	2001Q3	2001Q4	2003Q1	2003Q7

[a] Dates in parentheses are the NBER trough dates for each cycle.

9

Global Imbalances:
The Crisis That Did Not Occur . . . Yet

Francis E. Warnock

January 2010

Five years ago, global imbalances were held up as the primary cause of the next global financial crisis. A concise statement of the concerns at that time is provided in the opening paragraph of Roubini and Setser (2004), which analyzed the sustainability of US external deficits and the associated Bretton Woods Two international monetary system. Their paper examined

> . . . the sustainability of what Larry Summers has called the "balance of financial terror"—a system whose stability hinges on the willingness of Asian central banks to both hold enormous amounts of US Treasuries (and other US fixed income securities) and to add to their already enormous stocks to provide the ongoing financial flows needed to sustain the US current account deficit and the Bretton Woods Two system.

Roubini and Setser (2004) concluded "that the Bretton Woods Two system is fragile, and likely will prove unstable . . . the US is on an unsustainable and dangerous path." Feldstein (2006) laid out the risks associated with the large, bond-financed US current account deficit a bit more explicitly:

> This form of capital inflow poses a serious risk to the American economy. Foreign governments may decide to shift their funds from dollars to other currencies. Similarly, private investors who are current holders of US stocks and bonds may decide to make such

a shift. But they cannot collectively shift their funds out of dollars in the near term and cannot even reduce the flow of dollars to the United States. The trade deficit has to be financed and that requires a corresponding inflow of funds. To bring those funds would require higher rise in interest rates (or a fall in the value of the dollar). A shift in preferences away from the dollar could cause the interest rate in the US could rise rapidly. I don't have to tell you about the damage that would be caused by such a large rise in interest rates.

As it turned out, we did have a crisis, but not quite the one described in Roubini and Setser (2004) and Feldstein (2006). During the darkest moments of the crisis, global investors did not shun US assets; US interest rates (those on sovereign bonds, in particular) remained at historically low levels, and the dollar appreciated. That is not to say that global imbalances did not play a role in the crisis. To the extent they helped depress US long rates and provided additional demand for some assets now described as toxic, they almost surely added fuel to the fire. But a crisis involving foreign retrenchment from US bond markets, a sharp increase in US rates, and a plummeting dollar has not yet occurred.

On the heels of the recent financial crisis, it is worthwhile to step back and reassess global imbalances. While there are various lenses through which one can view global imbalances, I will do so from the perspective of global capital flows and international investment patterns. After reviewing current aspects of global imbalances, I will assess the trigger that could end global imbalances—US investors and the rest of the world fleeing US securities.

The Precrisis Period

A few years ago, the US current account deficit, while improving, was still at 5 percent of gross domestic product (GDP), a level that would trigger red flags to many observers. On a related note, the US consumer was an important driver of growth all over the world. In addition, emerging-market countries were acquiring enormous reserves (much of which ended up in US securities), US long-term interest rates were at historically low levels, and many countries were experiencing inflation rates not seen in decades. (See figures 9-1–9-4 for basic indicators through summer 2008.)

FIGURE 9-1

US CURRENT ACCOUNT BALANCE
(AS A PERCENTAGE OF GDP)

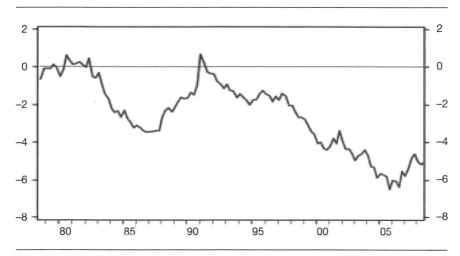

SOURCES: IMF and Haver Analytics.

FIGURE 9-2

TEN-YEAR US TREASURY YIELD
(AT CONSTANT MATURITY, PERCENT PER ANNUM)

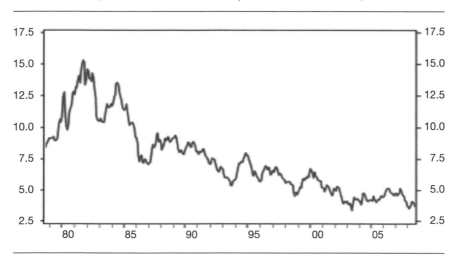

SOURCES: IMF and Haver Analytics.

FIGURE 9-3

TOTAL RESERVES (WORLD)

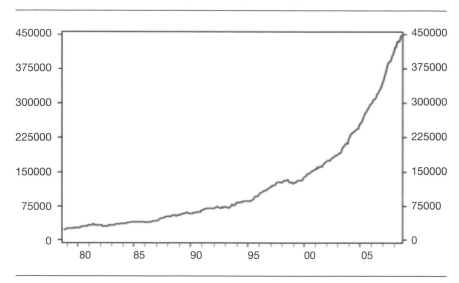

SOURCES: IMF and Haver Analytics.

FIGURE 9-4

CONSUMER PRICE INDEX (WORLD)

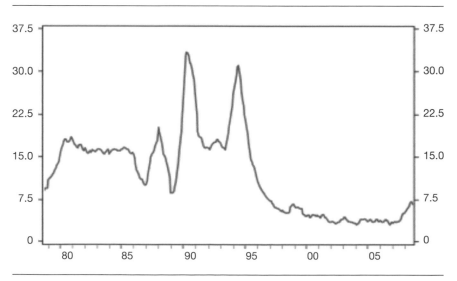

SOURCES: IMF and Haver Analytics.

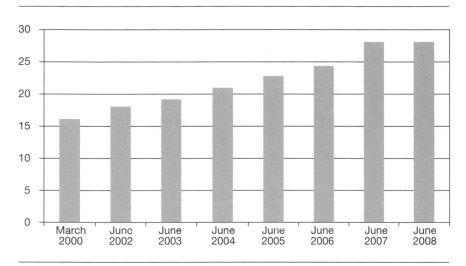

SOURCE: Author's calculations based on table 2 of http://www.treasury.gov/resource-center/data-chart-center/tic/Documents/shla2008r.pdf.

Many questioned the sustainability of this arrangement. An entire National Bureau of Economic Research book (Clarida 2007) explored issues related to large current account deficits in developed countries.

From my (admittedly narrow) perspective, exploding debt dynamics aside, sustainability hinged on foreigners' willingness to fund our current account deficits at something near the then-prevailing prices. And throughout much of the 2000s, they did: foreigners held an ever-increasing share of US debt securities, from 16 percent of the outstanding securities in 2000 to more than 25 percent by summer 2008 (see figure 9-5). For US Treasury bonds, the increase in foreign ownership was even more striking: foreigners held 35 percent of the Treasury bond market in 2000 and 61 percent—almost two-thirds of all Treasuries held by the public—by summer 2008. Were foreigners (or, for that matter, US investors) to decide that their portfolios were overstuffed with US securities—the trigger mentioned in Roubini and Setser (2004) and Feldstein (2006)—the dollar would fall, US long-term interest rates would spike, and global imbalances would decline.

The Crisis

Just when the discussion of global imbalances began to lose steam—foreigners' appetite for US securities had begun to seem almost limitless—the crisis hit. To be sure, this was not the external crisis predicted by those concerned about global imbalances. During the darkest moments of the crisis, the dollar appreciated and US long-term rates fell, directly counter to what would occur were this a global imbalances crisis.

But the financial crisis did hit, slowly at first, then gathering steam and in the process producing seismic shifts in global economic conditions. Global exports plummeted. The US current account deficit shrank because imports fell even faster than exports. With the dollar appreciating, there was little need for emerging-market governments to acquire reserves, and global reserves decreased for the first time in a decade. Global inflation, after peaking at 7 percent, fell to below 1 percent. Governments all over the world implemented massive stimulus packages.

The Postcrisis Era

Let us call the acute crisis period the fall of 2008, and the period since then the postcrisis era. This is not to suggest that we are out of the woods—many sizable economies around the world are out of the acute crisis period only because of massive governmental life support that brings its own set of problems.

Basic indicators have changed markedly. The US current account deficit has improved sharply. Emerging-market countries' acquisition of reserves, which paused during the crisis (while the dollar appreciated), has again surged. The dollar has resumed its decline against many currencies (but not against the renminbi). Global inflation has eased substantially. About the only constant is that US long-term interest rates remain at historically low levels. (See figures 9-6–9-9 for basic indicators through late 2009.)

We will view the postcrisis period with an eye toward how global imbalances—the crisis that did not occur—might play out going forward. We will focus on the roles of three types of investors: governments, other foreign investors, and US investors.

FIGURE 9-6

US CURRENT ACCOUNT BALANCE, 1980–2009Q3

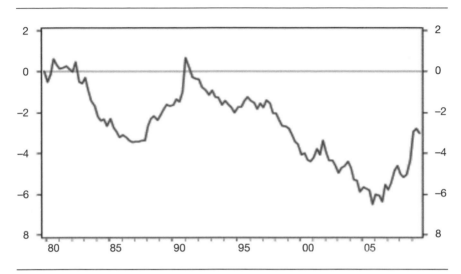

SOURCES: IMF and Haver Analytics.

FIGURE 9-7

TEN-YEAR US TREASURY YIELD, 1980–DECEMBER 2009

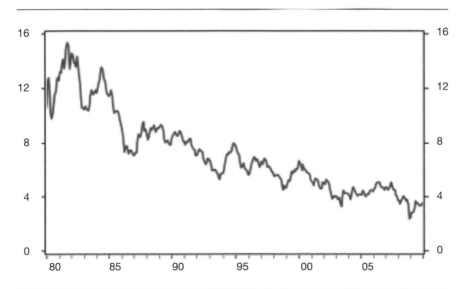

SOURCES: IMF and Haver Analytics.

FIGURE 9-8
TOTAL RESERVES (WORLD), 1980–OCTOBER 2009

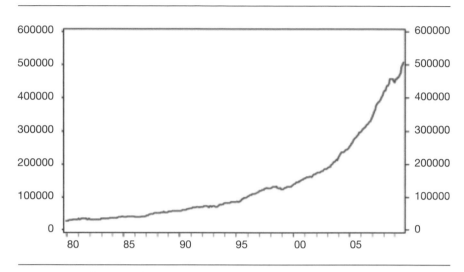

SOURCES: IMF and Haver Analytics.

FIGURE 9-9
CONSUMER PRICE INFLATION (WORLD), 1980–NOVEMBER 2009

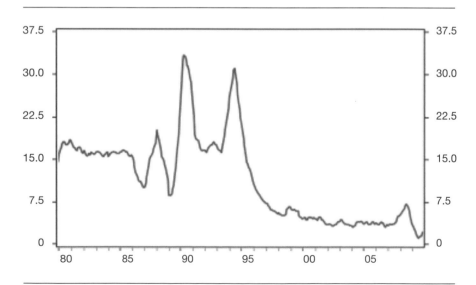

SOURCES: IMF and Haver Analytics.

Reserve Accumulation. In some sense, global imbalances can be seen as a choice variable for emerging-market governments, as the imbalances would not exist were it not for the exchange-rate policies of many emerging-market countries. Yes, the voracious appetite of the US consumer has been a necessary component of the imbalances—I am not discounting that side of the arrangement—but if emerging markets did not support the dollar, then a larger proportion of US spending would fall on domestic goods (because foreign goods would be more expensive). So one way of thinking about the likely path of global imbalances is to ask, "What would cause emerging-market governments to give up this arrangement?"

In the darkest period of the crisis, reserve accumulation paused, but it has since resumed and, indeed, surged (figure 9-8). To date there is little evidence that some of the major accumulators of reserves will be able (or willing) to rebalance their economies toward a greater emphasis on domestic demand. To the extent that a few key countries continue the accumulation of reserves to keep their currencies from appreciating—and, as noted, global reserves are again increasing—one basic driver of global imbalances will still be in play in the near term.

The massive reserve accumulation could end for at least two reasons. One, emerging-market countries could decide to focus on the development of domestic demand. I suspect that potential employment gains would be at the heart of this decision. Were it deemed that a shift to domestic demand could increase employment, we would be more likely to see such a shift. That said, to the extent that employment in export sectors is important, such a shift is unlikely. Two, reserve accumulation can be divisive *within* countries, in part because it is inflationary (and the poor bear the brunt of the impact of inflation). In 2007–2008, when world food prices experienced their sharpest rise in three decades, food riots swept through more than thirty countries, and governments in two countries (Haiti and Madagascar) were overthrown by the events set in motion by the price increases.[1] Moreover, reserve accumulation, which favors the export sector, can also increase inequality within a country. Were global inflation or strains between export sectors and other sectors to begin to rise again, one could imagine the citizens in emerging markets impressing on their governments the need to cease reserve accumulation.

The Nature of US Capital Flows

Global imbalances are also the result of choices made by US and foreign investors. Were US investors to increase their preference for foreign assets, or were foreigners to shy away from US assets, all else equal, the end of global imbalances would be nearer. Thus, another reasonable question is, "Has the crisis brought about a change in investors' preferences?"

The crisis has brought on a substantial shift in the composition of US capital flows, along with a dramatic reduction in gross flows. Interestingly, the United States is going through what, for a developed country, would be termed a current account reversal—the current account deficit has improved sharply over the past few years, with much of this improvement occurring in the past few quarters (figure 9-6). As noted in Freund and Warnock (2007), not all current account reversals are equal—those that in the buildup were financing consumption rather than investment are worse, and the recent US episode certainly falls into that category. Freund and Warnock also found that the type of inflows predominant in the buildup does not impact the extent of the subsequent adjustment. That is, in past current account reversals, the financial systems seemed to intermediate funds adequately, although it would be difficult to argue that case during the recent crisis.

Were the United States an emerging market, this episode would be called a sudden stop, not in the Calvo, Izquierdo, and Loo-Kung (2006) sense (in part because they have added a number of criteria to the definition of a sudden stop), but rather in the Rothenberg and Warnock (2011) "true sudden stop" sense. Gross financial inflows into the United States plummeted during the crisis (figure 9-10). Capital essentially stopped flowing into the country, a defining feature of a true sudden stop. The net impact of this sudden stop was muted by a massive decline in gross outflows; that is, US investors retrenched from global markets, thus mitigating the decrease in net inflows.

The figure shows, for both gross inflows and gross outflows, the difference in the four-quarter sum of flows (as a percentage of GDP) compared to the same sum a year earlier. During the crisis, gross inflows into the United States plummeted. Net inflows fell by much less as US investors brought money home (that is, gross outflows plummeted, although by slightly less than the drop in gross inflows).

FIGURE 9-10

US GROSS FINANCIAL INFLOWS AND OUTFLOWS

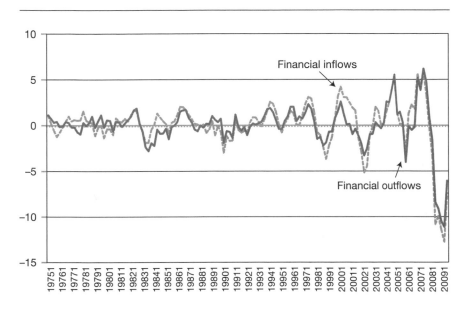

SOURCE: Author's calculations based on data from US Bureau of Economic Analysis.

NOTE: Last data point is 2009Q2.

The trigger Roubini and Setser (2004) and Feldstein (2006) worried about—a shift in global portfolios away from US securities—is still in play. With sharp increases in US public debt (figure 9-11), potentially adverse debt dynamics will give investors—both foreign and domestic—reason to think carefully before funding US budget deficits at anything near current interest rates.

Perhaps reflecting foreigners' concern, the share of US securities held by foreigners are estimated to have fallen in 2009 for the first time in at least a decade (table 9-1).

Accompanying this decline in foreign ownership of US securities have been striking changes in both the magnitude and composition of US financial flows (table 9-2). Net financial inflows (line 6), which slowed only slightly in 2008, fell sharply in 2009. This slowdown in net inflows masked a much sharper slowdown in gross financial inflows (line 14), which fell from an annual average of $1,744 billion before the crisis to only $534

FIGURE 9-11

US DEBT BY TYPE OF BORROWER

(AS A PERCENTAGE OF GDP)

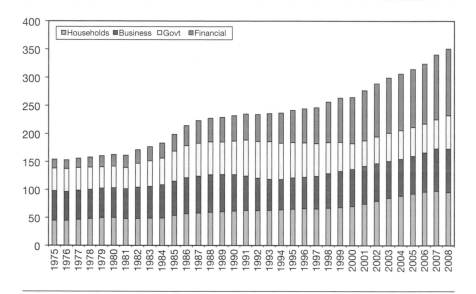

SOURCE: Author's calculations based on data from the Federal Reserve's *Flow of Funds Accounts.*

billion in 2008 and $377 billion (annualized) in the first three quarters of 2009. This slowdown in flows into US assets owed solely to the actions of private foreign investors (line 20); foreign official inflows (line 15) held up. The slowdown in private foreign flows into US assets owes to a newfound aversion to US agency bonds (line 25) and US corporate bonds (line 27). In the face of this true sudden stop, net financial inflows (line 6) held up in 2008 only because US investors' flows abroad (line 7) were zero.

Two reasonable questions: have we seen the peak in foreign ownership of US securities, and are zero US outflows likely to persist? It is reasonable to assume that foreigners, as they reexamine all asset classes in light of the crisis, will no longer purchase vast quantities of near substitutes to US risk-free assets. In the past, a large proportion of the inflows into the United States were in near substitutes to Treasury bonds (for example, agency bonds). Such flows seem unlikely to resume at past magnitudes. Once the crisis fully abates, one can imagine a resumption of foreign purchases of US corporate

TABLE 9-1
FOREIGN OWNERSHIP OF US LONG-TERM SECURITIES

	March 2000	June 2002	June 2003	June 2004	June 2005	June 2006	June 2007	June 2008	June 2009*
Equity									
Total outstanding	24,861	18,485	18,639	22,006	23,947	26,367	31,450	28,435	23,140
Foreign-owned	1,709	1,395	1,564	1,930	2,144	2,430	3,130	2,969	2,199
% foreign-owned	6.9	7.5	8.4	8.8	9.0	9.2	10.0	10.4	9.5
Marketable US Treasury									
Total outstanding	2,508	2,230	2,451	2,809	3,093	3,321	3,454	3,621	4,591
Foreign-owned	884	908	1,116	1,426	1,599	1,727	1,965	2,211	2,629
% foreign-owned	35.2	40.7	45.5	50.8	51.7	52.0	56.9	61.1	57.3
US government agency									
Total outstanding	3,575	4,830	5,199	5,527	5,591	5,709	6,202	6,986	7,243
Foreign-owned	261	492	586	619	791	984	1,304	1,464	1,273
% foreign-owned	7.3	10.2	11.3	11.2	14.1	17.2	21.0	21.0	17.6
Corporate and other debt									
Total outstanding	5,411	6,954	7,692	8,381	9,410	10,425	11,747	12,501	12,830
Foreign-owned	703	1,130	1,236	1,455	1,729	2,021	2,738	2,820	2,466
% foreign-owned	13.0	16.2	16.1	17.4	18.4	19.4	23.3	22.6	19.2
Total US long-term securities									
Total outstanding	36,355	32,499	33,981	38,723	42,041	45,822	52,853	51,543	47,804
Foreign-owned	3,557	3,925	4,502	5,430	6,263	7,162	9,137	9,464	8,567
% foreign-owned	9.8	12.1	13.2	14.0	14.9	15.6	17.3	18.4	17.9

SOURCE: Author's calculations based on table 2 of http://www.treasury.gov/resource-center/data-chart-center/tic/Documents/shla2008r.pdf.

NOTE: * = Author's estimates

TABLE 9-2

COMPOSITION OF US BALANCE OF PAYMENTS

(BILLIONS OF USD, ANNUALIZED)

		2004–2007	2008	2009	
1	Current Account Balance	−727	−706	−412	Sharp decrease in current account deficit.
2	Trade Balance	−697	−696	−359	Sharp decrease in trade deficit, as imports fell faster than exports.
3	Income Balance	70	118	78	
4	Current Transfers	−100	−128	−131	
5	Capital Account Balance	2	1	−3	
6	Financial Account Balance	667	534	138	Decrease in financial account balance.
7	US Outbound Flows	−1076	0	−239	US flows abroad plummeted to zero in 2008 and remain low.
8	US Direct Investment (DI) Abroad	−249	−332	−224	US DI abroad has maintained a reasonably high level.
9	US Flows into Foreign Securities	−288	61	−236	US investors sold foreign securities in 2008, but resumed net purchases in 2009.
10	Foreign Equities	−139	−1	−89	
11	Foreign Bonds	−149	62	−147	
12	US Flows into Foreign Banks	−541	806	−369	Net banking flows (i.e., when combined with inflows, below) positive in 2008, negative in 2009.
13	US Government Assets	2	−534	590	US government assets abroad unprecedentedly large, but across time sum to near zero.
14	US Inbound Flows	1744	534	377	Flows into the United States fell sharply in 2008 and remain low.
15	Foreign Official Inflows (FOI) into the United States	406	487	425	Foreign official inflows held up . . .
16	Treasury Securities	173	478	488	. . . as flows into Treasuries surged . . . .

17	Treasury Bonds and Notes	181	205	317	
18	Treasury Bills	-7	272	170	
19	Other FOI Inflows	233	9	-63	... offsetting the sharp decline in official purchases of agency bonds.
20	Private Flows into the United States	1337	47	-48	Private flows into the United States plummeted to zero in 2008 and were negative in 2009.
21	Foreign Direct Investment (FDI) in the United States	194	320	139	FDI in the United States held up ....
22	Treasury Securities	59	197	29	... but private flows into Treasuries, after surging in 2008, slowed sharply in 2009 ...
23	Treasury Bonds and Notes	47	13	53	
24	Treasury Bills	11	184	-24	
25	Agency Bonds	34	-185	-57	... and private foreigners now sell US agency bonds ...
26	US Equities	130	57	120	
27	US Corporate Bonds	367	1	-86	... as well as US corporate bonds.
28	Private Flows into US Banks	551	-372	-212	
29	Financial Derivatives	9	-29	.	
30	Statistical Discrepancy (SD)	49	200	250	Large positive SD suggests more net inflows and/or smaller current account deficit.

SOURCE: Author's calculations based on BEA's BOP data. (See "Interactive Tables: Detailed Estimates," http://www.bea.gov/international/index.htm#bop.)

NOTE: 2009 data are through Q3 (annualized).

bonds, although one would think that foreigners will have a greater appreciation of the risks inherent in such securities. Thus, a reasonable assessment is that flows into Treasuries will continue, although the magnitude is uncertain, especially given the current worries about potentially destabilizing debt dynamics; flows into corporate bonds should resume, although probably not at the heightened levels of the precrisis period; and flows into agency bonds will likely remain a trickle at best. That said, even if foreigners now have a greater appreciation of the risks associated with US debt, it is plausible that the United States could attract sizable equity and foreign direct investment (FDI) inflows, as it did through the tech boom and bust. However, with the US consumer likely to retrench, and the US government somewhat overextended and thus likely unable to put forward additional massive stimulus, the attractiveness of US equities is less than obvious.

Global imbalances will not persist if foreigners retreat from US markets. They will also not persist if another important but sometimes overlooked player—the US investor—leaves US markets and sharply increases positions in foreign markets. US investors' foreign-equity portfolios, which totaled $5.2 trillion at the end of 2007, have consistently (and significantly) outperformed global-equity benchmarks over the past two decades (figure 9-12). As investors naturally reassess asset classes in the aftermath of the crisis, one can imagine US assets looking somewhat less attractive relative to foreign assets; all else equal, this brings forward the endgame of global imbalances.

The Capacity of Non-US Markets to Absorb Sizable Capital Flows

While the above analysis suggests that there might be a surge in global investment away from US markets and toward foreign markets, it brings up a recurring question: what markets can handle the magnitude of global financial flows that would be unleashed in such a scenario? The euro area is a likely alternative. However, it is well known that the euro area does not currently provide a large, liquid market for a risk-free asset, as its sovereign-bond markets are not unified. The recent strains associated with Greece's downgrade highlight this point. China has begun conversations on possible alternatives to the US dollar as the international reserve currency. This would, presumably, involve a greater international role for the renminbi, but for now deep renminbi markets are years if not decades away. Other

FIGURE 9-12

PERFORMANCE COMPARISON:
US INVESTORS AND THE VALUE-WEIGHTED BENCHMARK
(EXCESS RETURNS, IN PERCENTAGE POINTS)

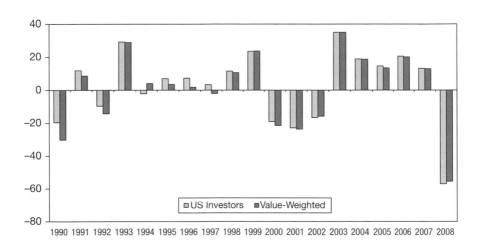

SOURCE: Curcuru et al. (2011).

NOTE: This figure depicts annual returns (in excess of a one-month eurodollar interest rate) for two portfolios. *Value-Weighted* is a benchmark portfolio based on MSCI market capitalization weights. *US Investors* is a portfolio based on US investors' holdings.

emerging markets (for example, Brazil) have shown the strains of large capital inflows and have responded with capital controls. Ten years ago, there was no viable alternative to the US dollar as the currency of the world's risk-free asset. Today, while the US risk-free market is less broad than investors previously believed, it is still not clear what the alternative is.

Conclusion

Global imbalances built up in the 2000s to such an extent that many thought they would bring on a global financial crisis that began with the rest of the world (and US investors) shunning US assets. As it happened, we had a global financial crisis, but not that one. In the darkest moments of the crisis, the dollar surged and US Treasury yields plummeted.

Global imbalances are building up again. The main question is, "What could trigger their cessation?" A benign trigger would be the cessation of massive reserve accumulation by some emerging markets, or an orderly shifting of global investors from US markets to other markets, although it is unclear which market could ultimately replace US markets on the global stage. A more malignant trigger would involve the dynamics presented by Roubini and Setser (2004) and Feldstein (2006): a sudden retreat of US and foreign investors from US markets that would bring about a sharp rise in US interest rates and a sharp decline in the dollar. The evidence suggests that while we are far closer to the trigger of a malignant ending to global imbalances, global investors' question of "if not the US, then where?" is still relevant.

References

Calvo, Guillermo A., Alejandro Izquierdo, and Rudy Loo-Kung. 2006. "Relative Price Volatility under Sudden Stops: The Relevance of Balance-Sheet Effects." *Journal of International Economics* 69: 231–254.

Clarida, Richard H. 2007. *G7 Current Account Imbalances: Sustainability and Adjustment.* Chicago: University of Chicago Press.

Curcuru, Stephanie E., Charles P. Thomas, Francis E. Warnock, and Jon Wongswan. 2011. "US International Equity Investment and Past and Prospective Returns." *American Economic Review* 101(7): 3440–3455.

Feldstein, Martin. 2006. "The Case for a Competitive Dollar: Remarks at the Annual SIEPR Summit." Stanford University, March 3.

Freund, Caroline, and Frank Warnock. 2007. "Current Account Reversals in Industrial Countries: The Bigger They Are, the Harder They Fall?" In *G7 Current Account Imbalances: Sustainability and Adjustment,* edited by R. Clarida, 133–162. Chicago: University of Chicago Press.

Rothenberg, Alexander D., and Francis E. Warnock. 2011. "Sudden Flight and True Sudden Stops." *Review of International Economics* 19(3): 509–524.

Roubini, Nouriel, and Brad Setser. 2004. "The US as a Net Debtor: The Sustainability of the US External Imbalances." Mimeo.

Note

1. See "If Words Were Food, Nobody Would Go Hungry," *The Economist,* November 21, 2009.

About the Contributors

Michael D. Bordo is professor of economics and director of the Center for Monetary and Financial History at Rutgers University. He has held previous academic positions at the University of South Carolina and Carleton University in Ottawa, Canada. He has been a visiting professor at the University of California Los Angeles, Carnegie Mellon University, Princeton University, Harvard University, and Cambridge University, where he was Pitt Professor of American History and Institutions. He has also been a visiting scholar at the International Monetary Fund, Federal Reserve Banks of St. Louis and Cleveland, the Federal Reserve Board of Governors, the Bank of Canada, the Bank of England, and the Bank for International Settlements. He is currently a national fellow at the Hoover Institution, Stanford University. He also is a research associate of the National Bureau of Economic Research. He has published many articles in leading journals and ten books on monetary economics and monetary history. He is editor of a series of books for Cambridge University Press, *Studies in Macroeconomic History*.

Ethan Ilzetzki is a lecturer (assistant professor) at the Department of Economics and an associate at the Center of Economic Performance at the London School of Economics. His research focuses on macroeconomics and fiscal policy, with a particular interest in macroeconomic policy in developing countries. He has held policy and research positions at the International Monetary Fund, the US Department of Treasury, and the Millennium Challenge Corporation.

181

Greg Ip is US economics editor for *The Economist*, based in Washington, DC. He covers the economy; financial markets; and monetary, fiscal, and regulatory policy. He contributes to *The Economist*'s blog, Free Exchange. He has commented frequently on radio and television, including CNBC, BBC, CNN, MSNBC, *PBS NewsHour* with Jim Lehrer, *Washington Week* with Gwen Ifill, and National Public Radio. He is the author of *The Little Book of Economics: How the Economy Works in the Real World* (Wiley, 2010). He joined *The Economist* in July 2008. Prior to his current job, Ip was a reporter for the *Wall Street Journal*, most recently as chief economics correspondent in Washington. He created Real Time Economics, the *Wall Street Journal*'s blog of Federal Reserve and economic news.

John Landon-Lane is an associate professor of economics in the Department of Economics, Rutgers University. He has published numerous journal articles and chapters in edited volumes in the areas of time series and Bayesian econometrics, macroeconomics, growth and development, and macroeconomic history. He has published a number of papers on the economic history of the United States, and his current research agenda includes a comparison of the recent global financial crisis to past global financial crises.

Enrique G. Mendoza is the Neil Moskowitz Professor of International Macroeconomics and Finance at the University of Maryland, which he joined in 2002. Before that, he held positions at the International Monetary Fund, the Board of Governors of the Federal Reserve System, and Duke University. He is also a research associate of the National Bureau of Economic Research, a former panel member of the National Science Foundation's Economics program, and has served on the editorial boards of six academic journals, including the *American Economic Review*. His research focuses on international capital flows, financial crises, sovereign debt, and international business cycles. His publications include articles in *Quarterly Journal of Economics*, *American Economic Review*, and *Journal of Political Economy*.

Frederic S. Mishkin is the Alfred Lerner Professor of Banking and Financial Institutions at the Graduate School of Business, Columbia University. He is also a research associate at the National Bureau of Economic Research, a member of the Squam Lake Working Group on Financial Reform, and the codirector of the US Monetary Policy Forum. From September 2006 to August 2008, he was a member (governor) of the Board of Governors of the Federal Reserve System. He has also been a senior fellow at the Federal Deposit Insurance Corporation Center for Banking Research and past president of the Eastern Economic Association. He has taught at the University of Chicago, Northwestern University, Princeton University, and Columbia University. He has also received an honorary professorship from the People's (Renmin) University of China. From 1994 to 1997, he was executive vice president and director of research at the Federal Reserve Bank of New York and an associate economist of the Federal Open Market Committee of the Federal Reserve System. His research focuses on monetary and regulatory policy and their impact on financial markets and the aggregate economy.

Vincent R. Reinhart is a managing director and chief US economist at Morgan Stanley. He is responsible for the firm's analysis of the US economy. For the four years prior to joining Morgan Stanley, Reinhart was a resident scholar at AEI. He previously spent more than two decades working in the Federal Reserve System, where he held a number of senior positions in the Divisions of Monetary Affairs and International Finance. For the last six years of his Fed career, he served as secretary and economist of the Federal Open Market Committee. In that capacity, he was the senior staff member providing advice to Fed officials on the appropriate choice and communication of monetary policy. In his research at the Fed and AEI, Reinhart worked on topics as varied as economic bubbles and the conduct of monetary policy, auctions of US Treasury securities, alternative strategies for monetary policy, the long-lived consequences of financial crises, and the patterns of international capital flows. At AEI, he frequently commented in the media on the economic outlook and macroeconomic and financial policies.

Ricardo Reis is professor of economics at Columbia University, where he teaches and does research in macroeconomics. He previously taught at Princeton University and has held visiting positions at Stanford University, Yale University, the University of Chicago, and the Russell Sage Foundation. Reis serves on the board of editors of several leading journals, is an affiliate of the National Bureau of Economic Research and the Center for Economic and Policy Research, and is an academic adviser and visiting scholar at the Federal Reserve Banks of New York and of Minneapolis. His current research investigates the role of fiscal automatic stabilizers in US recessions, the targeting of liquidity injections by central banks during crises, and the financial strength and exposure of central banks pursuing unconventional policies.

Angel Ubide is the director of global economics at Tudor Investment Corporation, a leading global funds management company, and a visiting fellow at the Peterson Institute for International Economics. He is an active member of several international economic policy organizations, including the Euro50 Group, the ECB's Shadow Governing Council, the Reinventing Bretton Woods Foundation, the Atlantic Council of the US, and the Center for European Policy Studies. He writes a biweekly column on international economics for *El Pais,* the leading Spanish newspaper, and contributes regularly to *Vox, Telos,* and *Aspenia.* Ubide has written extensively on international macroeconomics, banking, and exchange rates, and his work has been published in major international journals and leading newspapers. He was formerly an economist at the International Monetary Fund and a management consultant with McKinsey and Co.

Carlos A. Vegh is a professor of economics at the University of Maryland and a research associate at the National Bureau of Economic Research. He spent the early years of his career at the International Monetary Fund's Research Department. From 1995 to 2007, he was a tenured professor in UCLA's Department of Economics. He has been coeditor of the *Journal of International Economics* and the *Journal of Development Economics*, the leading journals in their respective fields, and has published extensively in leading academic journals on monetary and fiscal policy in developing and emerging countries. He has co-edited a volume in honor of Guillermo Calvo published by MIT Press and is currently working on a graduate textbook on open economy macroeconomics for developing countries, to be published by MIT Press.

Frank Warnock is Paul M. Hammaker Professor of Business Administration at the University of Virginia's Darden School of Business. His research,

which focuses on international capital flows, international portfolio allocation, and financial sector development, has been published in *American
Economic Review*, *Quarterly Journal of Economics*, *Journal of International Economics*, *Review of Financial Studies*, *Journal of Accounting Research*, and *Journal
of Housing Economics* (among other journals) and featured in *Financial Times*,
the *Economist*, *Barron's*, the *Wall Street Journal*, and the *New York Times*. At
Darden, Warnock has received multiple teaching awards and a Wachovia
Award for Research Excellence. Prior to joining Darden in 2004, he was
senior economist in the International Finance Division at the Board of Governors of the Federal Reserve System. He also taught at Georgetown University and the University of North Carolina. Warnock's current affiliations
include research associate at the National Bureau of Economic Research,
senior fellow at the Federal Reserve Bank of Dallas's Globalization and Monetary Policy Institute, and research associate at the Institute of International
Integration Studies at Trinity College Dublin. He also recently consulted
with the Bank for International Settlements on a project on housing finance
systems and with ShoreBank International on mobile banking in South Asia.

Christopher Whalen is senior managing director of Tangent Capital
Partners in New York, where he works as an investment banker providing
advisory services focused on companies in the financial services sector. He
is cofounder and vice chairman of the board of Lord, Whalen LLC, parent
of Institutional Risk Analytics, the Los Angeles–based provider of bank ratings, risk management tools, and consulting services for auditors, regulators, and financial professionals. He is also the author of the book *Inflated:
How Money and Debt Built the American Dream* (John Wiley & Sons, 2010).
He currently edits the *Institutional Risk Analyst*, a weekly news report and
commentary on significant developments in and around the global financial
markets. He also contributes articles to *Zero Hedge*, *Housing Wire*, and *The
Big Picture*. He is a fellow of the Networks Financial Institute at Indiana
State University, and a member of Professional Risk Managers' Interna-
tional Association. He was regional director of Professional Risk Managers'
International Association's Washington, DC, chapter from 2006 through
January 2010 and is a member of the Economic Advisory Committee of the
Financial Industry Regulatory Authority and the Global Interdependence
Center in Philadelphia.